D1636087

Teacher Manual

13th Edition

HUMAN GEOGRAPHY

Landscapes of Human Activities

Mark C. Jones

Mc
Graw
Hill

mheducation.com/prek-12

Send all inquiries to:
McGraw-Hill Education
8787 Orion Place
Columbus, OH 43240

ISBN: 978-0-07-697455-9
MHID: 0-07-697455-3

Printed in the United States of America.

3 4 5 6 7 8 QVS 23 22 21 20 19

About the Author

Mark C. Jones is a geographer in Manchester, New Hampshire. He has taught Advanced Placement Human Geography (APHG) at private schools and a variety of general education courses including Introduction to Geography at universities. Mark has scored APHG exams for many years. He has published articles about geography education, including lesson plans, in *Journal of Geography* and *The Geography Teacher*. His professional activities include past service on the steering committee of state geographic alliances, on the executive planning board of the National Council for Geographic Education (NCGE), and on the editorial board of the *Journal of Geography*. Mark earned a BA in International Relations from Bucknell University, an MA in Geography from Miami University, and a PhD in Geography from the University of Iowa.

Table of Contents

Chapter 1: Introduction: Some Background Basics   1

Chapter 2: Roots and Meaning of Culture: Introduction   9

Chapter 3: Spatial Interaction and Spatial Behavior   16

Chapter 7: Cultural Identities and Cultural Landscapes: Diversity and Uniformity   48

Chapter 8: Economic Geography: Primary Activities   55

Chapter 9: Economic Geography: Manufacturing and Services   64

Chapter 13: Human Impacts on the Environment   100

AP Human Geography Pacing Guide

Directions:

This is a suggested pacing guide for a Traditional (156 class periods until the AP Human Geography exam) and A/B Block (78 class periods until the AP Human Geography exam) school year based on the 7 units, or content areas, in the AP Human Geography Curriculum Framework. Some districts might have more or less days, so some adjustment might be necessary. A simple suggestion is that you should be finished with Political Patterns and Processes by winter break, and with all content early enough to allow 2-3 weeks for in-class review for the exam.

UNIT 1	Thinking Geographically
Traditional	12 days
A/B Block	6 days
Chapters	Chapter 1: Introduction: Some Background Basics
	Chapter 13: Human Impacts on the Environment

UNIT 2	Population and Migration Patterns and Process
Traditional	20 days
A/B Block	10 days
Chapters	Chapter 3: Spatial Interaction and Spatial Behavior
	Chapter 4: World Patterns, Regional Trends
	Chapter 13: Human Impacts on the Environment

UNIT 3	Cultural Patterns and Processes
Traditional	20 days
A/B Block	10 days
Chapters	Chapter 2: Roots and Meaning of Culture: Introduction
	Chapter 5: Language and Religion: Mosaics of Culture
	Chapter 6: Ethnic Geography: Threads of Diversity
	Chapter 7: Cultural Identities and Cultural Landscapes: Diversity and Uniformity

UNIT 4	Political Patterns and Processes
Traditional	22 days
A/B Block	11 days
Chapters	Chapter 12: The Political Ordering of Space

UNIT 5   Agriculture and Rural Land-Use Patterns and Processes

Traditional   22 days

A/B Block   11 days

Chapters   Chapter 8: Economic Geography: Primary Activities

Chapter 13: Human Impacts on the Environment

UNIT 6   Cities and Urban Land-Use Patterns and Processes

Traditional   22 days

A/B Block   11 days

Chapters   Chapter 11: Urban Systems and Urban Structures

Chapter 13: Human Impacts on the Environment

UNIT 7   Industrial and Economic Development Patterns and Processes

Traditional   20 days

A/B Block   10 days

Chapters   Chapter 9: Economic Geography: Manufacturing and Services

Chapter 10: Economic Development and Change

Chapter 13: Human Impacts on the Environment

Using the AP Teacher Manual

This AP Teacher Manual is designed to help you plan for teaching AP Human Geography. The elements included in each chapter are suggestions on how to encourage your students to engage with the course content. While the activities presented are by no means exhaustive, they provide a launch point for you to tailor the course to your own classroom.

Our activities are designed with diverse classrooms in mind. Some activities may work better for larger or smaller classes. In all cases, we have tried to ensure that the supporting resources we suggest are widely available at no cost. We hope that this will ensure that all students, regardless of institutional resources, will be able to access these assets.

Each chapter begins with an **Introduction** to the chapter concepts and will allow you to quickly see the AP Enduring Understandings from one or more of the seven units, or content areas, outlined in the Curriculum Framework that will be important to cover for the chapter.

The **Concepts and Themes** section contains a chapter overview as well as a list of AP Learning Objectives from the Curriculum Framework. Both allow you to quickly orient yourself to each chapter. **Key Words** provides a list of important terms students will need to know, with AP-specific terms given added emphasis. In some cases, a **Note to the Teacher** provides more detailed explanation of terms to help you extend that content to the class.

The **Chapter Discussion and Activities** section provides suggestions for incorporating the chapter's information into the classroom and identifies the AP Essential Knowledge statements from the Curriculum Framework that are addressed in each activity.

The **Chapter Feature Answer Keys** provide teachers with answers and guidance on using the *Geography and Citizenship* feature in the text. Many of the questions accompanying each feature focus on writing and argument, as discussed in the AP Course Description for Human Geography.

Test Practice Answer Keys are included in every chapter. The questions in the Test Practices reflect the multiple-choice questions (MCQs) and free-response questions (FRQs) on the actual AP Exam. Scoring notes on the latter are included to make grading easier and more informative.

About the AP Human Geography Course

We cannot promise any "magic formula" to ensure your students score well on their Advanced Placement Human Geography Exam, but this book can help. Human Geography is exciting, and it will help students better understand the society in which they live, making them more informed citizens.

The purpose of this introduction is two-fold. The first section provides an overview of the goals of the AP Course and AP Exam, helping you to understand the basic format of the exam and the rationale behind its structure and format. The section offers a series of strategies and tips meant to help you prepare your students for the major sections of the exam.

Purpose and Scope of the Examination

The Advanced Placement Course is meant to replicate a college-level introductory Human Geography course and thus give students the skills and knowledge for more specialized courses in Geography. While there are an infinite variety of ways to present an AP Course, there are certain things that every student should get out of his or her course. These include an understanding of the patterns and processes that have shaped our knowledge, use, and modification of the Earth. In addition, students should come out of an AP Course with certain skills, including the ability to critically analyze primary and secondary sources; to develop a thesis or argument and support it with concrete evidence; and to examine human spatial organization and its environmental consequences, as well as the methods and tools geographers use, that are vital to understanding Human Geography.

The College Board and Educational Testing Service, which administer the AP Exam, surveyed over 100 college and university instructors across the country to get a sense of what is being taught in introductory college survey courses. A Test Development Committee, which consists of three college or university professors and three high school teachers, uses this information to create an examination that reflects the experience that most undergraduate students receive. It is administered in mid-May. The AP Human Geography Exam is then scored by a group of thousands of AP high school teachers, and college and university professors who serve as AP Exam Readers. These teachers gather for a week in early June and receive training in how to score the exam, and then spend the rest of the week reading and scoring student essays.

Colleges and universities often grant credits equivalent to that which is offered for their introductory Human Geography course to those students who successfully complete the AP Exam. The criteria for receiving credit vary widely from institution to institution, and students should find out from each college and university what their standards are. Students may also choose to have their scores sent to colleges and universities to which they are applying. The AP Exam is scored on the following 5-point scale: 5 is "extremely well qualified"; 4 is "well qualified"; 3 is "qualified"; 2 is "possibly qualified"; 1 is "no recommendation."

Examination Format

There are two sections to the Advanced Placement Human Geography Examination: a multiple-choice section (Section I) and a free-response section (Section II). The free-response section consists of 3 essay questions. The examination lasts for two hours and fifteen minutes, with one hour for multiple choice and one hour and fifteen minutes for the essays (the breakdown is explained further in the following paragraphs). The multiple-choice questions make up 50% of the final score and the free-response questions make up the other 50%.

Multiple Choice

Students have one hour to answers the multiple choice questions. The multiple-choice questions include defining, explaining, and applying geographic concepts and interpreting geographic data. Each multiple-choice question will have five answer options. Even if students do not know the answer they should be encouraged to take their best guess as points are not deducted for incorrect answers.

Free Response

Students have one hour and fifteen minutes to devote to the three essay questions. The three essays require students to demonstrate an understanding of models, to analyze and evaluate geographic concepts, to cite and explain examples of geographic processes, and to analyze geographic patterns, relationships, and outcomes in applied contexts. Students should spend about one-third of their time on each of the three essays and use their analytical and organizational skills to craft their responses in narrative form. If an essay prompt is separated in to parts, students should supply a separate narrative for each part.

Thinking About the Examination

One indispensable resource to help you prepare your students for the AP Exam is the College Board's AP Central website (apcentral.collegeboard.org). The AP Central Human Geography section includes sample questions from the past several years, along with sample student responses and scoring explanations. In addition, it includes the College Board's Course Description.

Many people often look to past years to see if they can "guess" what the upcoming free-response questions might be. This is rarely successful. To reiterate what we said earlier, the best way to prepare for the AP Exam is to teach the fundamental concepts of Human Geography as expressed in the AP Curriculum Framework. Students will not know every concept equally well, but the degree of choice on the standard essay should allow them to find questions that they feel comfortable answering. Similarly, their knowledge and spatial thinking skills should enable them to navigate a free-response question on any topic.

Basic AP Human Geography Advice for Students

Prepare for the exam—good luck and providence play but a small role in achieving a good score on the AP Exam.

Get to the exam site early with all the equipment you need (tissues, pencils and pens, and a watch).

Get plenty of sleep the night before—napping during the exam is not recommended.

Have fun—you have worked hard to learn about the patterns and processes of human geography—this is an opportunity to excel, be creative—you have nothing to lose and everything to gain.

CHAPTER 1
Introduction: Some Background Basics

AP Introduction

Chapter 1 is a broad overview of geography as a discipline and contains foundational concepts that will be referenced throughout the book. Chapter 1 correlates with the first content area of the College Board's AP Human Geography (hereafter APHG) curriculum framework, Unit 1 Thinking Geographically. Chapter 1 addresses the following AP Enduring Understandings from the APHG course framework:

- Geographers use maps and data to depict relationships of time, space, and scale.
- Geographers analyze relationships among and between places to reveal important spatial patterns.
- Geographers analyze complex issues and relationships with a distinctively spatial perspective.

Sequence and Pacing

While the College Board does not insist that the APHG teacher cover the units in the order shown in the course framework, that order represents a logical progression of topics. Each unit makes more sense because of the units previously completed. For example, given the importance of cultural patterns in shaping the global system of states, many of which are nation-states or have boundaries which reflect the importance of language and religion in establishing communities, it makes sense to address cultural geography (Unit 3) before political geography (Unit 4).

Teachers should allocate the available weeks of instruction time in roughly equal amounts to the seven units of the APHG course framework. The first unit contains vital perspectives that, if understood well by the students, will make learning the other six units considerably easier. If you are offering APHG for the first time and/or your students are in grades 9 and 10, you may wish to allocate slightly more days to the first unit. As you and your students gain experience with the course and thinking geographically, the class may be able to move slightly faster with the later units.

AP AP Concepts and Themes

Chapter Overview

This chapter contains fundamentals of geography as a discipline, including the following:

- Essentials of map types and their use
- How geographic data is collected
- Uses of geographical data
- Basic concepts in spatial relationships
- How humans and the environment influence each other
- Using scales of analysis to reveal spatial patterns
- Spatial thinking using regions as organizing constructs

Learning Objectives

- Identify types of maps, the types of information presented in maps, and different kinds of spatial patterns and relationships portrayed in maps.
- Identify different methods of geographic data collection.

- Explain the geographical effects of decisions made using geographical information.
- Define major geographic concepts that illustrate spatial relationships.
- Explain how major geographic concepts illustrate spatial relationships.
- Define scales of analysis used by geographers.
- Explain what scales of analysis reveal.
- Describe different ways that geographers define regions.

Key Words

Use the terms below with a ▌to focus your study of AP Human Geography key words in this chapter.

▌absolute direction

▌absolute distance

▌absolute location

accessibility

administrative region

▌cartogram

cartography

▌choropleth map

▌clustering

concentration

connectivity

cultural landscape

density

develop

▌dispersion

▌dot map

▌environmental determinism

equator

field

▌formal region

▌functional region

geographic feature

▌geographic information system (GIS)

▌global positioning system (GPS)

globalization

▌graduated circle (symbol) map

graphic scale

graticule

human geography

▌isoline map

latitude

longitude

▌projection

mental (cognitive) map

meridian

model

natural landscape

▌natural resource

object

parallel

▌pattern

▌perceptual (or vernacular) region

physical geography

▌place

place stereotype

placelessness

▌possibilism

prime meridian

proportional area symbol

raster approach

▌reference map

region

regional concept

regional geography

▌relative direction

▌relative distance

▌relative location

▌remote sensing

representative fraction

scale

▌scale of analysis

site

situation

▌space

spatial diffusion

spatial distribution

spatial interaction

spatial system

statistical map

systematic geography

▌thematic map

thematic region

vector approach

Note to the Teacher

The Key Words *environmental determinism* and *possibilism* are included in the AP Course Framework for Unit 1, but these concepts are not discussed in depth in the Bjelland Student Edition until Chapter 2, pages 37–38.

The Key Word *scale of analysis* appears in the AP Course Framework but is not called out as a Key Word in the Bjelland Student Edition. In the context of human geography, a *scale of analysis* is a framework for understanding how events and processes at different scales influence one another. The questions asked by geographers, and the answers arrived at, are dependent upon the scale of analysis. For example, the closing of an auto manufacturing plant in Ohio may be the result of global economic forces rather than a dip in the state or local economy.

AP Chapter Discussion and Activities

Identifying Bad Maps

AP ESSENTIAL KNOWLEDGE: All maps are selective in information; map projections inevitably distort spatial relationships in shape, area, distance, and direction.

TEACH: *To assist students in becoming more sophisticated users of maps, ask them to find a "bad" map. Some students may need a quick reminder that bad maps are difficult to read or understand because of the use of certain colors and fonts, the scale used to create the map, or the organization and accuracy of data on the map.*

Students might find examples of bad maps in many locations, but advertising flyers, newspapers, and magazines sometimes contain maps that are candidates for criticism. After each student has found at least one example, have them take turns sharing the maps with the class. Evaluate each map in a class discussion. Ask students to consider why the map is ineffective or misleading.

Understanding Difficulties in Map Reading

AP ESSENTIAL KNOWLEDGE: Types of spatial patterns represented on maps include absolute and relative distance and direction, clustering, dispersal, and elevation.

TEACH: *Ask students why they think some Americans encounter difficulty in reading a map by considering the following questions: Has the easy availability of GPS-enabled devices including cars and cell phones caused the average citizen to lack the ability to understand a map? If not the proliferation of GPS, then what else is to blame? Encourage students to share their thoughts and opinions in a class discussion.*

Collecting and Organizing Spatial Data

AP ESSENTIAL KNOWLEDGE: Spatial information can come from written accounts in the form of field observations, media reports, travel narratives, policy documents, personal interviews, landscape analysis, and photographic interpretation.

TEACH: *Have students practice gathering and organizing data by researching the country of origin of items of clothing. Work as a class to pick 30–50 items of clothing and record the country of origin or the country of final assembly. Items of clothing can include shirts, pants, coats, and footwear. Students can use their own clothing, or they can search online stores to find this information.*

After collecting the data, ask students to consider how the data can be organized to reveal something they did not know about geography and economics. What might reveal a spatial pattern? For example, students may suggest that the data can be organized by country to show the types of clothing manufactured in a certain country or region of the world. Note that this data can be retained for reuse during the unit on economic geography.

Using Absolute and Relative Location

AP ESSENTIAL KNOWLEDGE: Spatial concepts include absolute and relative location, space, place, flows, and pattern.

TEACH: *Ask each student to create two sets of directions for walking or driving from their home to the school—one using absolute location and one using relative location. As they complete the activity, have students think about what makes each type of location useful when giving directions. Which type of location seems more useful? How do students' directions differ? What may be the reasons for differences? Discuss students' answers as a class.*

Analyzing Human-Environment Interaction

AP ESSENTIAL KNOWLEDGE: Concepts of nature and society include sustainability, natural resources, and land use.

TEACH: *Ask students to scan the mass media at the national, state, and local scales of analysis for current examples of human-environment interaction. Students should be looking for instances of how humans influence the natural environment, as well as instances in which humans are influenced by nature.*

As they read the news, ask students to answer the following questions in a one-page essay: How important or significant is the influence of humans on the natural world? Are the human impacts on the environment favorable, neutral, or unfavorable as they pertain to the best interests of society?

Understanding Scales of Analysis

AP ESSENTIAL KNOWLEDGE: Scales of analysis include global, regional, national, and local.

TEACH: *Explain to students that the United States uses a federal system of government with power shared between the national (federal), state, and local governments. To illustrate how scales of analysis are interconnected, ask students to select an issue in contemporary American society and explain how the three levels of government (three scales of analysis) interact. Students should share their thoughts in an oral presentation. To wrap up this activity, discuss with students how the concept of scales of analysis can be transferred to the study of geography.*

Defining Regions

AP ESSENTIAL KNOWLEDGE: Regions are defined on the basis of one or more unifying characteristics or on patterns of activity.

TEACH: *Remind students that regions are defined by one or more unifying characteristic. Regions can then be further divided into sub-regions. For example, the United States is a region of the larger world. Within the U.S. region, there are sub-regions like the Northeast, the South, the Midwest, and the West.*

Give students the following challenge: Using your state, county, or city/town as the region, sketch, name, and describe the sub-regions you believe exist. What characteristic(s) help you recognize the sub-regions shown in your map? Once each student has created his/her own sketch map, ask students to share their criteria for defining the regions on their maps.

AP Test Practice Answer Key

Below are the Bjelland end-of-chapter AP Test Practice questions along with their answers, feedback, and rubrics.

Multiple Choice Questions

1. The importance of analyzing landscapes such as the one in the Figure 1.1 on page 3 is that it

   (A) provides a context for understanding human-environment relationships.

   (B) allows geographers to make assumptions about the impact of climate change.

   (C) has an impact on government policy about the environment.

   (D) explains why people spend large amounts of money on leisure activities.

   (E) shows how leisure activities in developing countries compare to those in developed areas.

   Answer: A
   Feedback: Landscape analysis allows geographers to look at the environment in real life or in a photograph and study the impact of human beings on that environment. It is not necessarily about the impact of climate change (although it could be) and it does not always have an impact on government policy. While the photo shows people engaged in a leisure activity, it does not make a judgment as to whether people spend lots of money on them, and there is no way to compare developed and developing countries based on the photo.
   Chapter: 1. Introduction: Some Background Basics
   Section: 1.1
   AP Topic: 1.5 Human Environmental Interaction

2. A major difference between relative space and absolute space is that

(A) relative space is the area where groups or family members live while absolute space is not inhabited by a person's relations.

(B) relative space is made up of the places a person goes to on a day-to-day basis.

(C) relative space is comparative and varies with context, while absolute space is based on mathematical coordinates.

(D) absolute space is more often used by geographers to show relationships between places.

(E) absolute space is less accurate than relative space for showing location.

Answer: C
Feedback: Absolute space is based on mathematical coordinates such as latitude and longitude, not on whether one's relatives live there or where one travels in that space. Geographers use both relative and absolute space to show the relationships between places, and absolute space is more accurate for showing location.
Chapter: 1. Introduction: Some Background Basics
Section: 1.2
AP Topic: 1.1 Introduction to Maps

3. Looking at maps at different scales, such as the population density maps in Figure 1.9 on page 11, is important for a geographer because

(A) density changes within an area as the scale is made smaller or larger.

(B) information that is true at a larger scale may not be true of all areas at a smaller scale.

(C) small-scale maps are often less accurate than large-scale maps.

(D) large-scale maps allow information to be tailored to the county or city level.

(E) conclusions from large-scale studies can be assumed to be true at smaller scales as well.

Answer: B
Feedback: Answer B is correct because information at a smaller scale shows nuances of the data that are important to geographers. Simply saying that billions of people live in China does not show that very few of those people live in the desert or mountainous parts of that country. Using a large-scale map to show that a state voted for a specific political candidate may be less important than seeing that the large population of one city in that state swung the vote away from the candidate voted for by the sparsely populated rest of the state.
Chapter: 1. Introduction: Some Background Basics
Section: 1.2
AP Topic: 1.1 Introduction to Maps

4. A local TV or radio station's broadcast area, a pizza shop's delivery area, and a neighborhood church are all examples of functional (or nodal) regions because

(A) they have a specific function in the neighborhood.

(B) they are all regulated by local government laws.

(C) they have relationships with areas outside their own locality.

(D) they are small-scale businesses.

(E) they have a central location and are only available within a specific area.

Answer: E
Feedback: A functional (nodal) region has a center such as the radio antenna, the pizza shop, or the church. It is only used by people within a certain radius of that center point. Go outside that area and the radio station will not come in, the pizza shop will not deliver, and the drive to the church will be too far. It does not have a relationship with areas outside its region. Many things have a function within the neighborhood or are regulated by the government without being a functional region. Some functional regions can be quite large, so they are not all small businesses.
Chapter: 1. Introduction: Some Background Basics
Section: 1.2
AP Topic: 1.7 Regional Analysis

5. In order to make a series of map overlays to show the interaction of terrain with city infrastructure, a geographer would use

(A) a GPS system.

(B) a cartogram.

(C) a polar projection.

(D) a GIS system.

(E) an urban model.

Answer: D

Feedback: A GPS system is used to find a specific point on the map, such as in your car or smart phone. A cartogram is a kind of map that shows the amount of a phenomenon in an area rather than the correct size and shape of the area. A polar projection shows the earth as it looks from one of the poles, and urban models show how cities are laid out geographically. The correct answer, a GIS system, makes a series of maps that can be laid on top of one another to see relationships between them.

Chapter: 1. Introduction: Some Background Basics

Section: 1.4

AP Topic: 1.2 Geographic Data

6. A problem with studying geography by region is

(A) regions may overlap and often have transitional boundaries.

(B) regions are so different from one another that comparisons are impossible.

(C) functional regions are no longer a valid concept in human geography.

(D) some regions are more developed than others.

(E) climate regions play a very important role in agricultural practices.

Answer: A

Feedback: Answers B and C are incorrect because geographers often compare regions and they often use the concept of functional regions. While D and E are both true, they are not a problem associated with studying geography by region.

Chapter: 1. Introduction: Some Background Basics

Section: 1.2

AP Topic: 1.7 Regional Analysis

7. All of the following are ways that mapping spatial data is used to analyze the human organization of space EXCEPT

(A) dot matrix maps, which use a dot to represent a specific amount of data on a map.

(B) thematic maps, which can show the distribution of specific phenomena or the spatial characteristic of numerical data.

(C) topographical maps, which show the elevation of an area along with the landscape features added by humans.

(D) choropleth maps, which use gradations of color to show a spatial characteristic of specific data.

(E) cartograms, which show the number of instances of a specific phenomenon by graphing it on an X and Y axis.

Answer: E

Feedback: A, B, C, and D are all true. Answer E, cartograms, are also a way of mapping spatial data, but they are not graphed on an X-Y axis. They are a kind of map.

Chapter: 1. Introduction: Some Background Basics

Section: 1.3

AP Topic: 1.1 Introduction to Maps

8. When describing the location of a place on the earth, geographers use

(A) site to explain the physical characteristics of a place and situation to explain the place's relationship to other places.

(B) latitude and longitude to note the relative location of the place on the globe.

(C) place names and other toponyms to describe the place.

(D) absolute and relative distance to describe location based on where other nearby places are located.

(E) cultural landscape studies to compare that place's location to other places on the earth.

Answer: A

Feedback: Answer A, site and situation, are two ways that geographers describe location. They also use latitude and longitude, but these mark absolute, not relative location. Answer C is not totally wrong since place names or toponyms can be used to describe a location, but they are problematic since many places can have the same name (Columbus, GA, and Columbus, OH, for example). D is also possible but is not a very accurate way of locating a specific place on the earth. The cultural landscape is influenced by the geographic location but comparing places on the earth culturally does not influence the geographic location.

Chapter: 1. Introduction: Some Background Basics

Section: 1.2

AP Topic: 1.4 Spatial Concepts

9. The two photographs of Miami, Florida, in Figure 1.12 on page 14 illustrate the idea that

(A) the physical landscape of an area never changes.

(B) human impact has had a major impact on the physical landscape in the past but what people do today has had little impact.

(C) rising population has very little impact on the physical landscape.

(D) the characteristics of a place today are a result of the impact humans have had on their physical landscape in the past.

(E) geography is only useful for studying the physical landscape of the past.

Answer: D

Feedback: A, B, C, and E are all false. Physical landscape often changes either naturally (from floods, earthquakes, volcanoes, etc.) or because of human activity in the past or today (mining, building roads, damming rivers, etc.). As populations grow, humans have more and more impact on the landscape. Geographers study the physical landscape of the past and of the present. So the correct answer is D, the landscape and characteristics of a place today are the accumulation of all the things that have been done in the past.

Chapter: 1. Introduction: Some Background Basics

Section: 1.2

AP Topic: 1.5 Human Environmental Interaction

10. Field experiences for human geographers are

(A) a way that data was gathered before the advent of GIS and GPS systems.

(B) a way that organizations and individuals can gather useful data for economic, environmental, and social decision making.

(C) studies that focus on rural areas and agricultural data collection.

(D) made by doing controlled experiments in laboratories.

(E) only used to study developing countries through interviews, photographs, informal observations, and surveys.

Answer: B

Feedback: Work in the field is a major part of a geographer's work, allowing him or her to gather data on both rural and urban areas in developing and developed countries outside of a laboratory setting. The data, once it is collected, might be transferred to a GIS mapping system to see relationships between various types of data. It would not be used with a GPS system. The correct answer is B, which states organizations and individuals then use field experience data for decision-making purposes.

Chapter: 1. Introduction: Some Background Basics

Section: 1.2

AP Topic: 1.2 Geographic Data

Free Response Questions

1. Answer Parts A, B, and C below.

(A) Define the term *cognitive* or *perceptual region* (also called a *vernacular region*) and give an example.

(B) Define the term *mental map* and explain how one might be used.

(C) In what ways are mental maps similar to perceptual regions?

(A) A vernacular or perceptual region is one that is defined differently by different people. The term *the South*, for example, can be defined in various ways. It might simply mean the area of the country that is to the south of where you live, but it could also mean the area of land that supported the Confederacy during the Civil War, which southerners often call "Dixie." The area that many people refer to as "downtown" can have various meanings.

(B) A mental map is a person's unique view of spatial reality that relies on landmarks important to him or her. We rely on mental maps every time we travel from one place to another without the aid of outside information. We use mental maps to give directions to others when we tell them to go to the gas station and turn left to get to the store.

(C) Both mental maps and perceptual regions are representations of the ways humans think about where they are located on the earth. Perceptual regions tend to be about how a group of people thinks about a location, while mental maps are unique to each individual. However,
both types of thinking involve more than one interpretation of the same geographic area.

Rubric: This question is worth six points. In Part A, a point is given for defining the term and another point is for the example. In Part B, the
definition gets one point and the explanation of how it could be used gets a second point. In Part C, two points are awarded for the comparison
of the two ideas—one point if the comparison is simply stated and a second point for the explanation.

Chapter: 1. Introduction: Some Background Basics

Section: 1.2 and 1.4

AP Topic: 1.7 Regional Analysis

2. Look at the map in Figure 1.5 on page 9 to answer Parts A, B, and C.

(A) Name the type of projection shown and explain why this projection might be used by a geographer.

(B) Name another type of projection. Explain what this type of projection could be used for and what
the drawbacks of using it could be.

(C) Name a third type of projection, for what it could be used, and possible drawbacks of using it.

(A) The Polar projection on page 9 is shown from the perspective of looking down at the earth from the North Pole. It would be useful to see
the relationship between the continents from this angle, so a geographer could study how various countries interact. For example, as the
polar ice melts, ships and trade will be able to navigate across the north of Canada and Russia.

(B) Another type of projection is the Mercator projection, which was originally made to help ships navigate across oceans. This projection has
latitude and longitude lines that are straight and meet at right angles which is useful for navigation. However, it distorts the size and shape
of landmasses at the poles.

(C) A third type of projection is an Interrupted projection, which keeps the size and shape of continents correct but cannot be used to calculate
distance since pieces of the map have been cut out of the oceans. (The student might use a Peters projection, a Robinson projection, or
another as a third example.)

Rubric: This essay is worth eight points, two points for letter A (name of projection and use), and three points each for B and C (type, use, and
drawback).

Chapter: 1. Introduction: Some Background Basics

Section: 1.2

AP Topic: 1.1 Introduction to Maps

3. Answer Parts A, B, and C below.

(A) Define the terms *spatial distribution* and *spatial association*.

(B) Explain the difference between arithmetic density and physiological density. How does density
affect the spatial distribution of a phenomenon?

(C) How do dispersion (or concentration) and pattern affect the spatial distribution of a phenomenon?

(A) Spatial distribution refers to the arrangement of items on the Earth's surface while spatial association refers to the relationship between
various spaces.

(B) Arithmetic density is the number of something on a specific area of land (people, for example, per square mile). Physiological density is the
number of people on a specific area of arable land. This has to do with spatial distribution because of the relationship between the number
of people and the amount of land able to be farmed will predict whether there might be a famine.

(C) Dispersion/concentration and pattern affect the spatial distribution of people on the land because two areas with the same population may
have very different concentrations or patterns. All the people might be clustered in one area, or they might be more spread out. They might
form a pattern if they all live near a river or a highway.

Rubric: This essay is worth seven points. The student would get two points for A, one each for the definitions of the terms. Three points would
be awarded for B, one each for the definitions of *arithmetic density* and *physiological density*, and one for its relationship to spatial distribution.
Two points would also be awarded for C, one each for explaining how dispersion and pattern affect the spatial distribution of a phenomenon.

Chapter: 1. Introduction: Some Background Basics

Section: 1.2

AP Topic: 1.1 Introduction to Maps

Roots and Meaning of Culture: Introduction

AP Introduction

Chapter 2 introduces students to the concepts of culture, including many ways geographers think about the spatial dimension to learned behavior. Chapter 2 focuses on the third content area of the College Board's AP Human Geography curriculum framework, Unit 3 Cultural Patterns and Processes. Chapter 2 addresses the following AP Enduring Understandings from the AP Human Geography course framework:

- Cultural practices vary across geographical locations because of physical geography and available resources.
- The interaction of people contributes to the spread of cultural practices.
- Cultural ideas, practices, and innovations change or disappear over time.

AP Concepts and Themes

Chapter Overview

This chapter contains fundamentals of the study of cultural geography, including the following:

- Human culture takes varying forms across space
- The visible imprint of culture upon the surface of the earth is the cultural landscape
- Culture traits spread across space as a result of different types of diffusion

Learning Objectives

- Define the characteristics, attitudes, and traits that influence geographers when they study culture.
- Describe the characteristics of cultural landscapes.
- Explain how landscape features and land and resource use reflect cultural beliefs and identities.
- Define the types of diffusion.
- Explain how historical processes impact current cultural patterns.

Key Words

Use the terms below with a ▌ to focus your study of AP Human Geography key words in this chapter.

▌ acculturation

artifact

carrying capacity

▌ contagious diffusion

cultural autonomy

cultural convergence

cultural divergence

cultural ecology

cultural integration

▌ cultural landscape

cultural system

▌ culture

culture complex

▌ culture hearth

culture realm

culture region

▌ culture trait

diffusion

domestication

environmental determinism

▌ expansion diffusion

▌ hierarchical diffusion

hunter-gatherer

ideological subsystem

independent invention

innovation

mentifact

multilinear evolution

possibilism

▌ relocation diffusion

sociofact

sociological subsystem

▌ stimulus diffusion

▌ syncretism

technological subsystem

Note to the Teacher

The Key Word *stimulus diffusion* appears in the AP Course Framework but is not called out as a Key Word in the Bjelland Student Edition. As defined in human geography, *stimulus diffusion* occurs when an innovation is rejected in its original, complete form, but an aspect of the innovation is eventually adopted by the local culture.

AP Chapter Discussion and Activities

Identifying the Impact of Physical Geography on Culture

AP ESSENTIAL KNOWLEDGE: Cultural traits include such things as food preferences, architecture, and land use.

TEACH: *To help students appreciate the role of physical geography in shaping the culture of a place, ask each student to select a part of the world that he or she knows relatively little about. Students should conduct research to learn about the place they selected. They should then focus on determining key aspects of the natural environment including climate, topography, vegetation, and potential natural resources, such as metals, hydrocarbons, plants, fish, etc. Then students should learn something of the society or societies who live in the place they selected.*

As students conduct research, have them consider the following questions: In what ways does this culture reflect adaptation to the physical environment? Has this culture group attempted to modify the environment to their advantage or to suit their way of life? Have students create a visual presentation to share their findings that addresses these questions. A class discussion can follow to compare and contrast the places students researched.

Interpreting Cultural Landscapes

AP ESSENTIAL KNOWLEDGE: Cultural landscapes are combinations of physical features, agricultural and industrial practices, religious and linguistic characteristics, evidence of sequent occupancy, and other expressions of culture including traditional and postmodern architecture and land-use patterns.

TEACH: *Explain that the cultural landscape can serve as a historical record of the peoples who have occupied a place or region. The built landscape and toponyms in a place or region are clues as to which culture groups occupied that space and what was important to that society. Ask students to select a place to interpret its cultural landscape. The place selected could be a small town, a neighborhood within a larger community, or a region within a country. Depending on the size of the study area selected, students could combine review of a map with a personal exploration of the place.*

Once students have selected an area of study, have them gather information about the cultural land-scape through field research or online and library research. Encourage them to use photographs to illus-trate examples of the cultural landscape they studied. Then discuss students' findings as a class. If students are walking or driving around their selected study area, remind them to be aware of their personal safety while evaluating a place.

Understanding How Diffusion Affects Culture

AP ESSENTIAL KNOWLEDGE: Cultural ideas and practices are socially constructed and change through both small-scale and large-scale processes such as urbanization and globalization. These processes come to bear on culture through media, technological change, politics, economics, and social relationships.

TEACH: *Discuss with students how popular culture presents opportunities to learn about how behaviors and products diffuse within a society. Ask each student to pick an innovation such as an expression, consumer product, or technical process like distributing information. Then tell students to write a brief essay to answer these questions about their selected innovation: From its point of origin, how does it diffuse? Is the innovation spread by a single form of diffusion or a combination of forms? Are there any barriers which inhibit the spread of the innovation?*

Categorizing Types of Diffusion

AP ESSENTIAL KNOWLEDGE: Relocation and expansion—including contagious, hierarchical, and stimulus expansion—are types of diffusion.

TEACH: *To help students appreciate the differences among the various types of diffusion, draw a tree chart graphic organizer with the word* diffusion *at the top. The two types of diffusion are relocation and expansion, each of which can be shown below but connected to the word* diffusion. *The three subtypes of expansion diffusion are contagious, hierarchical, and stimulus. These can be added below but connected to the word expansion.*

Have students copy this graphic organizer onto a piece of paper. Then ask them to come up with one real world example of each type of diffusion and add it to their graphic organizer. The resulting graphic organizers, after being checked for the accuracy of the examples, can be shared among the students to illustrate the types of diffusion with corresponding examples.

AP Test Practice Answer Key

Below are the Bjelland end-of-chapter AP Test Practice questions along with their answers, feedback, and rubrics.

Multiple Choice Questions

1. All of the following are components of culture EXCEPT

(A)   the language spoken in an area.

(B)   the tools and technology people use.

(C)   religion and other shared beliefs.

(D)   types of food, shelter, and clothing found in an area.

(E)   the migration of people from one area to another.

Answer: E
Feedback: Culture is made up of practices, technologies, attitudes, and behaviors transmitted by societies. The migration of people from one place to another will bring a new culture into an area, but it is the process, not the culture itself.
Chapter: 2. Roots and Meaning of Culture: Introduction
Section: 2.1
AP Topic: 3.1 Introduction to Culture

2. The Burning Man Festival in the Black Rock desert of Nevada is an example of

(A)   national culture found in the United States.

(B)   regional culture of the desert Southwest.

(C)   Native American culture that has become popularized.

(D) a subculture of shared practices, technologies, attitudes, and behaviors.

(E) a random group who takes over the area once a year to play music and make works of art.

Answer: D

Feedback: A subculture is the practices, technologies, attitudes, and behaviors of a group of people within another culture. Latino-American and Native American subcultures exist within the United States, for example. The fact that people who go to Burning Man adhere to a specific set of beliefs and rules while making creative art and music qualifies them as a subculture.

Chapter: 2. Roots and Meaning of Culture: Introduction

Section: 2.1

AP Topic: 3.1 Introduction to Culture

3. The spread of religious ideas as people migrate to new areas is an example of

(A) relocation diffusion.

(B) expansion diffusion.

(C) hierarchical diffusion.

(D) contagious diffusion.

(E) stimulus diffusion.

Answer: A

Feedback: Religious ideas can be spread in many ways, by a king like Henry VIII forcing his people to convert (hierarchical diffusion) or by televangelists on TV and the internet spreading their ideas (contagious diffusion). Sometimes part of a religion spreads while other parts do not (stimulus diffusion). However, the question specifically asks about religion spreading as people migrate, which is the definition of relocation diffusion.

Chapter: 2. Roots and Meaning of Culture: Introduction

Section: 2.7

AP Topic: 3.4 Types of Diffusion

4. An example of cultural influences on a population's health can be seen in

(A) the discovery of new cures for cancer.

(B) UN workers vaccinating babies in developing countries.

(C) the number of doctors and hospital beds per capita.

(D) government provision of universal health care.

(E) patterns of obesity in the Deep South.

Answer: E

Feedback: The answer to this question must reflect cultural influences on a specific population. Answers A and C are simple facts that do not have to do with culture specifically. Answers B and D do not reflect a specific culture of an area. Answer E is correct because it names a specific area which has cultural traits that lead to obesity. The southern propensity for eating high fat, often fried foods, is an example of a cultural trait that causes health issues in that region.

Chapter: 2. Roots and Meaning of Culture: Introduction

Section: 2.7

AP Topic: 3.2 Cultural Landscapes

5. The spread of Christianity in Europe is an example of hierarchical diffusion because

(A) it spread from the nobility down to the peasants.

(B) it was spread through the migration of Christians from the Middle East to Europe.

(C) it spread from Rome to more provincial areas.

(D) it was a grassroots movement that mainly appealed to the poor.

(E) rulers and more educated people were able to read religious texts.

Answer: C

Feedback: Hierarchical diffusion spreads from more important or powerful areas or people to those with less importance and power. Answer A is simply false. Nobles did not spread Christianity, and while B and E might be true, they are not examples of hierarchical diffusion. Answer C is correct because Rome was a major city of great importance in the ancient world and from there, Christianity spread to the provinces and the Roman Empire grew.

Chapter: 2. Roots and Meaning of Culture: Introduction

Section: 2.7

AP Topic: 3.7: Diffusion of Religion and Language

6. Because of the phenomenon of friction of distance,

   (A)   cultures tend to change more quickly as they move farther from the hearth.

   (B)   the farther away people are from one another, the more similar their cultures will be.

   (C)   the farther away two areas are from one another, the more interaction they have.

   (D)   populations that are close to one another geographically may experience more barriers that hinder interaction.

   (E)   culture and technology in one area may spread more quickly to other nearby areas.

Answer: E

Feedback: The definition of *friction of distance* is that "areas which are nearer to one another are more likely to interact with one another and thus have more influence." This is the opposite of Answer C, which also makes A and B untrue. D is also false. As a rule, there are fewer barriers the closer areas are to one another.

Chapter: 2. Roots and Meaning of Culture: Introduction

Section: 2.8

AP Topic: 3.8 Effects of Diffusion

7. The Masai of Kenya and Tanzania disdain any job unrelated to herding cattle, but they also measure wealth by ownership of cattle and eat a diet that includes milk and cow blood. Together, these aspects of culture make up a

   (A)   subculture.

   (B)   culture complex.

   (C)   culture region or realm.

   (D)   national culture.

   (E)   cultural ecology.

Answer: B

Feedback: A set of cultural traits shown by members of the same group is called a cultural complex. A subculture is a small group of people within a larger group who all show a set of traits in common. Thus, a subculture exhibits a cultural complex. A cultural region or realm is a larger group of people, while national culture is the beliefs of an entire country. Cultural ecology is the study of the relationship between the group of people and its natural environment.

Chapter: 2. Roots and Meaning of Culture: Introduction

Section: 2.1

AP Topic: 3.3 Cultural Patterns

8. The two photographs in Figure 2.17 on page 51 show

   (A)   the impact of traditional agricultural techniques on advanced cultures.

   (B)   the fact that developed countries are able to grow much more food than developing countries.

   (C)   the use of traditional artifacts in developing countries as contrasted to the use of advanced technology in developed countries.

   (D)   the importance of animals in developing countries, while developed countries no longer have animals on farms.

   (E)   that farmers in developing countries work much harder than those in developed countries.

Correct Answer: C

Explanation: Answer A is false, and while B is true, it does not actually answer the question. Answer D is also false. There are animals on farms in developed countries, although many farms now specialize in either crops or livestock and the animals are not used in place of machines. Answer E is a stereotypical kind of thought that students need to be careful to avoid. Farmers in all countries must work hard many hours a day in all kinds of weather. The two photos do show the contrast between farming in developing and developed countries, one of the hallmarks of which is the traditional methods in the former and the more advanced technology in the latter.

Chapter: 2. Roots and Meaning of Culture: Introduction

Section: 2.6

AP Topic: 3.2 Cultural Landscapes

9. The photographs of people wearing various types of clothing in Figure 2.19 on page 53 illustrate the concept that

   (A) religious differences are evidenced mainly through the clothing worn by adherents of various faiths.

   (B) the purposes of clothing in a society can be to make a fashion statement, to protect the wearer, to delineate a person's job or status, or to meet a requirement of a person's culture.

   (C) people make value judgments based on the clothing worn by members of their society.

   (D) people in more traditional societies wear clothing that is required by their cultures, while people in developed countries do not.

   (E) the wearing of certain clothing is not at all influenced by geography.

   Correct Answer: B
   Explanation: The correct answer is B, that clothing serves many purposes in a society. Answer A is incorrect. The main religious differences are in belief, not in what clothing people wear. People do make value judgments based on how members of their society dress as in C, but this is not what is being shown by the photographs. Answer D is incorrect. People in all societies wear clothing that is required of them, as evidenced by the uniforms of police and soldiers. Answer E is also incorrect since climate and material for clothing will always affect what people wear.
   Chapter: 2. Roots and Meaning of Culture: Introduction
   Section: 2.6
   AP Topic: 3.1 Introduction to Culture

10. A major difference between traditional and more modern societies is that

    (A) modern societies adapt to new ideas rapidly while traditional societies change more slowly or not at all.

    (B) modern societies reject innovation while traditional societies recognize its value.

    (C) hunter-gatherers, who lived in equilibrium with their surroundings, needed to innovate quickly in order to survive.

    (D) innovation has very little impact on the culture of traditional people.

    (E) larger urban centers tend to reject innovation while more rural communities embrace it.

    Answer: A
    Feedback: Traditional societies tend to stay the same, reject change, or change more slowly than modern societies, which contain urban areas that are centers of innovation and change. Innovation has a large impact on traditional people when they do embrace it, changing their culture radically.
    Chapter: 2. Roots and Meaning of Culture: Introduction
    Section: 2.7
    AP Topic: 3.6: Contemporary Causes of Diffusion

Free Response Questions

1. Use your own knowledge, as well as the map in Figure 2C on page 58, to answer the following questions.

   (A) Using the concepts of *hearth* and *distance decay*, explain the distribution of Walmart stores shown on the map.

   (B) Explain another example of the phenomenon of hearth and distance decay.

   (C) Define *friction of distance* and explain its impact on diffusion.

   (A) The hearth is where a phenomenon begins, in this case the first Walmart. It began in the southeastern United States and then diffused (spread) outward from there. As it moved farther from the hearth into neighboring states and across the country, Walmart stores are fewer in number. This is distance decay (the idea that there is always less of something the farther away it is from the hearth).
   (B) Another example of this would be eating rice. The hearth of rice is in East Asia, therefore people in China, Korea, and Japan eat much more rice than people in South America. People in South America eat a lot of corn and potatoes, which were first grown in that region.
   (C) Friction of distance means that two areas that are near one another tend to have more interactions than areas that are farther apart. The fact that there is much more influence of Hispanic culture in the southwestern United States, which is near Mexico, than there is Hispanic culture in Maine is an example of friction of distance.
   Rubric: This question is worth six points, one for hearth, one for distance decay, two for another example and explanation, and two more for the definition and explanation of friction of distance.
   Chapter: 2. Roots and Meaning of Culture: Introduction
   Section: 2.7
   AP Topic: 3.8: Effects of Diffusion

2. Answer Parts A, B, and C below.

    (A) Define the term *syncretism*.

    (B) Name and explain two examples of syncretism.

    (C) Explain the impact of syncretism on the culture of a country.

(A) Syncretism occurs when a religion or other new idea comes into an area and is merged with an old idea that was already there.

(B) The voodoo religion is a good example of this, when Native American, African and Catholic religions mixed on islands in the Caribbean. This has an impact on the culture of the area since many people practice voodoo along with going to Catholic church services. Another example of syncretism is that when ethnic restaurants open in the United States, these restaurants change their recipes and presentations of food to appeal to American palates and culture. Taco Bell does not make authentic Mexican style food, which is often spicier than Americans would like. Panda Express does not make "real" Chinese food either. In China, for example, people do not get fortune cookies after a meal. People can get chopsticks to eat with, however, which is an authentic part of Chinese culture.

(C) One impact of syncretism is that, while a new group coming into an area begins to assimilate to the old culture, there is a blurring of lines between the cultures which allows the two to get along with one another.

Rubric: This answer is worth seven points. One point is given for the definition of *syncretism*. The student receives a point for each example given and another point for each explanation of the example. Two more points are given for the explanation of the impact of syncretism.
Chapter: 2. Roots and Meaning of Culture: Introduction
Section: 2.8
AP Topic: 3.8: Effects of Diffusion

3. Explain how natural barriers, political barriers, and social barriers can inhibit the spread of culture, giving examples of each.

There are many barriers that inhibit the spread of culture between areas. Some barriers are natural, such as oceans or high mountain ranges. The Himalayas, for example, made cultural diffusion between Chinese and Indian cultures difficult for centuries. Japan was able to pursue a policy of isolation for many years because it is a chain of islands. Japan is also a good example of a political barrier, since its government specifically worked to keep the islands isolated from foreign influences, resulting in a unique Japanese culture. Government immigration restrictions, such as those between the United States and Mexico, inhibit the exchange of cultures. Socially, religious and cultural taboos can inhibit the exchange of culture. So, too, can religious fanaticism, such as the restrictions placed on the Afghan people by the Taliban. The adherence of Quebec to the French language has meant that its culture has not spread much in neighboring English-speaking areas.

Rubric: This question is worth six points, two each for the natural, political, and social barriers discussed. Naming a barrier without explaining it would gain the student one point for each part. The second point is for each explanation.
Chapter: 2. Roots and Meaning of Culture: Introduction
Section: 2.8
AP Topic: 3.3: Cultural Patterns

CHAPTER 3
Spatial Interaction and Spatial Behavior

AP Introduction

Chapter 3 introduces students to essential ideas concerning how people and places interact across space, with considerable attention given to migration. The AP Human Geography course framework does not include a chapter specific to spatial interaction. Rather, a limited number of concepts and examples pertinent to spatial interaction are found among a few AP Human Geography units including Unit 2 Population, Migration Patterns and Processes. Chapter 3 addresses the following AP Enduring Understandings from the AP Human Geography course framework:

- Geographers analyze relationships among and between places to reveal important spatial patterns.
- Geographers analyze complex issues and relationships with a distinctively spatial perspective.
- Changes in population are due to mortality, fertility, and migration, which are influenced by the interplay of environmental, economic, cultural, and political factors.
- Cultural ideas, practices, and innovations change or disappear over time.
- The presence and growth of cities vary across geographical locations because of physical geography and resources.
- Economic and social development happen at different times and rates in different places.

AP Themes and Concepts

Chapter Overview

This chapter contains fundamentals of the study of spatial interaction and spatial behavior in geography, including the following:

- Looking at the world spatially
- Studying place to reveal underlying spatial patterns
- Changes in population are partially the result of migration behavior
- Migration can be voluntary or involuntary and occur in various forms

Learning Objectives

- Define major geographic concepts that illustrate spatial relationships.
- Explain how major geographic concepts illustrate spatial relationships.
- Describe different ways that geographers define regions.
- Explain factors that account for contemporary and historical trends in population growth and decline.
- Explain how different causal factors encourage migration.
- Describe types of forced and voluntary migration.
- Explain historical and contemporary geographic effects of migration.
- Communication technologies, such as the Internet and the time-space convergence, are reshaping and accelerating interactions among people; changing cultural practices, as in the increasing use of English and the loss of indigenous languages; and creating cultural convergence and divergence.
- Explain the processes that initiate and drive urbanization and suburbanization.
- Explain causes and geographic consequences of recent economic changes, such as the increase in international trade, deindustrialization, and growing interdependence in the world economy.

Key Words

Use the terms below with a ▌ to focus your study of AP Human Geography key words in this chapter.

activity space	▌internally displaced person	▌Ravenstein's laws of migration
▌asylum seeker	intervening opportunity	▌refugee
attitude	law of retail gravitation	Reilly's Breaking-Point Law
awareness space	link	reluctant relocation
barrier	▌migration	remittance
behavior	migration field	▌rural-to-urban migration
behavioral approach	mobility	▌space
▌(Christaller's) Central Place Theory	movement bias	▌space-time compression
▌chain migration	natural hazard	space-time path
channelized migration	network	space-time prism
cognition	network bias	spatial interaction
▌complementarity	node	spatial search
counter (return) migration	partial displacement migration	▌step migration
critical distance	▌pattern	temporary travel
▌dispersion	personal communication field	▌territoriality
distance decay	personal space	time geography
First Law of Geography	place perception	total displacement migration
forced migration	place utility	transferability
friction of distance	potential model	▌transhumance
▌gravity model	▌pull factor	voluntary migration
▌guest worker	▌push factor	

Note to the Teacher

The following Key Words appear in the AP Course Framework but are not called out as Key Words in the Bjelland Student Edition.

- *asylum seeker:* A person who seeks political refuge (asylum) in a country other than their own due to fear of harassment, imprisonment, or even death caused by the government.

- *guest worker:* A migrant permitted to work in a country other than their homeland due to a temporary labor shortage. The best-known example of the use of guest workers when West Germany invited people from Turkey in the aftermath of World War II.

- *internally displaced person* (IDP): An IDP is a person who has had to leave their home community due to the danger caused by environmental catastrophe, civil unrest, or war, but has not sought refuge in another country.

- *rural-to-urban migration*: A very common type of migration, particularly in economically developing countries, whereby people leave the countryside for a major city's greater opportunities in employment, education, health care, etc.

- *transhumance*: A type of nomadic migration in which herders move their flock between grazing areas according to the season.

- *Ravenstein's laws of migration*: E.G. Ravenstein, a British demographer, studied internal migration in England in the nineteenth century. Based on his data, he proposed several laws of migration. Many of these laws are still relevant today. These laws are: Most migrants only travel a short distance.; Migrants who travel longer distances usually move to big cities.; Most migration proceeds step by step.; Most migration is rural to urban movement.; Every migration flow results in a return migration, or counter-flow.; Most migrants are adults, and families are less likely to migrate internationally.; Most international migrants are adult males.

Understanding Complementarity and Interaction

AP ESSENTIAL KNOWLEDGE: Complementarity and comparative advantage establish the basis for trade.

TEACH: *Explain that complementarity exists when goods available in one location are needed in, affordable to, and able to be transported to another location. Have students think about the goods and services produced by their home state(s) or their region within a state. Then have a class discussion using the following questions: Where does your state's or region's exports go? This could be to other U.S. states or to other countries. From where does your state's or region's imports come? If needed, encourage students to use online resources to help them answer these questions. Discuss examples of complementarity that emerge.*

Understanding Causes of Migration

AP ESSENTIAL KNOWLEDGE: Migration is commonly divided into push factors and pull factors.

TEACH: *To help students move from abstraction to reality in studying migration behavior, ask them to research the personal migration of a family member, neighbor, or community member who has moved multiple times over several decades. Have students consider the following questions during their research: Where did this person live? Why did his or her move occur? Which were more important in the move—push factors or pull factors? Did an intervening opportunity change the intended destination for any of that person's moves? Discuss students' findings as a class. What patterns can they identify? Students may come to realize that immigration, life cycle, and career path considerations often cause people to move.*

Identifying Pull Factors of Migration

AP ESSENTIAL KNOWLEDGE: Push/pull factors and intervening opportunities/obstacles can be cultural, demographic, economic, environmental, or political.

TEACH: *Remind students that going away to college is an example of a temporary migration. In addition to the characteristics of the college they will attend, students must consider the characteristics of the community and region surrounding the college. Discuss the following question with the class: In planning your temporary migration to college, what types of information do you need to obtain about the community and ways to travel there?*

Analyzing Migration

AP ESSENTIAL KNOWLEDGE: *Social, cultural, political, and economic factors influence fertility, mortality, and migration rates.*

TEACH: *A useful skill for students to have in learning to think critically is to be able to develop a typology (study of types) for any one phenomenon. Ask students to create a typology, or classification, of voluntary migrations, including examples from recent years. Students' typologies can be in an annotated list format or in a more visual format, such as a chart or a graphic organizer. Discuss students' typologies as a class to identify similarities and differences.*

Tell students that the reasons people move differ greatly and may be more diverse than they realize. A partial list of examples of voluntary migrations includes: religious pilgrimages, humanitarian relief, moving closer to family to help relatives in need, attending a higher education institution, retiring in an interesting locale, etc.

Understanding Forced Migration

AP ESSENTIAL KNOWLEDGE: Forced migrations include slavery and events that produce refugees, internally displaced persons, and asylum seekers.

TEACH: *Explain that some of the most prominent examples of mass migration are forced migrations, both historic and contemporary. These include the trans-Atlantic slave trade (16th–19th centuries), the expulsion of Native American groups from the southeastern United States (early 19th century), and Russian and later Soviet governments sending political opponents to prison camps in Siberia (18th–20th centuries). More recently— beginning in 2011 and reaching a high point in 2015—there has been the movement of millions of Syrians fleeing civil war for safety in Europe.*

Ask students to make posters with both historic and contemporary examples of forced migrations. Some outside research may be necessary. Posters should be set up in two columns—one for historic and one for contemporary examples. Students should identify the push factor(s) that forced large numbers of people to flee their country of origin. Such push factors could be political oppression, cultural/religious discrimination, economic crisis, environmental catastrophe, or widespread crime. In selecting both historic and contemporary examples of forced migrations, students should attempt to include examples with different root causes from diverse countries and time periods.

AP Chapter Feature Answer Key

Geography and Citizenship

1. Research papers include correct grammar, style, and punctuation, and present students' findings using clear, logical organization. Research papers should also reflect students' understanding of the issues.

2. Students' position papers should reflect an understanding of the issue and defend their position with logical, supporting evidence. Encourage students with opposing opinions to share their thinking with the class.

3. Students' answers will vary, and may include popular but not necessarily true statements students may have heard from their parents, peers, the media, etc. Be sure that students are educating themselves with correct information on this topic.

4. Presentations should reflect logical reasoning and an understanding of this issue, and should include visuals and other supporting information to defend their reasoning.

5. Student pairs should work together to research and debate this issue. Remind students that they might not personally agree with or support the side they're arguing, but that they should be able to logically defend a stance using their research findings.

6. Students' paragraphs should reflect an understanding of this issue.

7. Students' position papers should clearly and logically defend their position on this issue.

AP Test Practice Answer Key

Below are the Bjelland end-of-chapter AP Test Practice questions along with their answers, feedback, and rubrics.

Multiple Choice Questions

1. Study Figure 3.3 on page 66. The reason people behave as they do when a new shopping mall opens is because

    (A) the new mall is more modern and therefore would be cleaner and have nicer shops, so more people go to it.

    (B) the new mall is similar to the old mall, so there is no change in consumer behavior.

    (C) the new mall is nearer and so more people will go to it.

    (D) people will continue to be loyal to the old mall that they have shopped at for years.

    (E) young people will go to the new mall, while older people will continue to shop at the old mall.

    Answer: C

    Feedback: According to the phenomenon of friction of distance, the fact that the new mall is nearer will make more of a difference than other factors in determining where people shop. While some people might remain loyal and some might be affected by the modernity of the new mall, the majority will shop at the one closest to them.

    Chapter: 3 Spatial Interaction and Spatial Behavior

    Section: 3.1

    AP Topic: 6.1 The Origin and Influences of Urbanization

2. The concept of space-time compression (or convergence) affected U.S. cities

(A) when cars and expressways were introduced in the first half of the 20th century, allowing goods to be more easily brought in from farther away.

(B) when the use of modern time-keeping methods and time zones were introduced in the mid-19th century.

(C) when commute times became longer due to traffic problems, making it necessary for commuters to live close to their work in the late 20th century.

(D) when the development of supersonic transport made it possible for goods to be sent long distances extremely quickly.

(E) when truck and rail shipments became more expensive, causing prices to rise in the inner cities.

Answer: A

Feedback: The term *space-time compression* (or convergence) means that things seem closer to one another because it takes less time to travel between them. The distance between Europe and the United States seems closer now than it did in the past because now we can take an airplane and fly there in just a few hours instead of taking a weeks-long ship voyage.

Chapter: 3. Spatial Interaction and Spatial Behavior

Section: 3.1

AP Topic: 3.5 Contemporary Causes of Diffusion

3. According to the gravity model

(A) the amount of interaction between two cities is based on the amount of resources available in those places.

(B) the amount of interaction between two cities is based on the distance between them.

(C) the amount of interaction between two cities is based on the type of work done in each.

(D) the amount of interaction between two cities is based on the size of the cities and the distance between them.

(E) the amount of interaction between two cities is based on the available transportation.

Answer: D

Feedback: The gravity model is an important one to know but it is not necessary to know the actual formula for the AP test. It states that the interaction between areas depends upon the size of the city (whether measured by population, amount of trade produced, or another method) divided by the distance and then multiplied by a constant k. The closest correct answer to this model is D. Resources, distance, type of work, and availability of transportation are all important, but none is the deciding factor by itself.

Chapter: 3. Spatial Interaction and Spatial Behavior

Section: 3.1

AP Topic: 6.1 The Origin and Influences of Urbanization

4. Each person's activity space includes all of the following EXCEPT

(A) territoriality, the emotional attachment to a specific place one sees as home.

(B) a zone of privacy and separation of others called personal space.

(C) the area in which we go about our normal daily routine, which is our activity space.

(D) the stage of life space, which differs depending on whether we are a child, an adult, or an elderly person.

(E) the awareness space, or an individual's assessment of the possibility of locations outside the normal realm of activity.

Answer: D

Feedback: The four types of space are territoriality, personal space, activity space, and awareness space. A person's stage of life influences his or her activity space since children are often not allowed to go to certain places, adults have many time/space constraints due to work and childcare, and the elderly may not be able to travel as they once did. Other things affect activity space as well, such as gender roles and accessibility of transportation.

Chapter: 3. Spatial Interaction and Spatial Behavior

Section: 3.3

AP Topic: 1.4 Spatial Concepts

5. From a time-geography perspective, all of the following are true of women's lives EXCEPT

    (A) women are frequently disadvantaged due to multiple work, child care, and home maintenance tasks.

    (B) women on average make more—though shorter—trips while men make longer but less frequent trips.

    (C) women face limitations in their choices of employment or other activities outside the home due to time-budget restrictions.

    (D) women who are single parents experience more constraints than do women who have other adults in the household to share tasks.

    (E) single women with no children experience the most time-budget restrictions.

Answer: E
Feedback: Studies, such as the one by Mei-Po Kwan, show that women who have children are constrained by the myriad household and childcare restrictions placed upon them. Because of time-budget constraints, they may have to take less well-paying jobs that are nearer to their homes and child care. Women who have another adult in the home who can shoulder some of the childcare, errands, and housework experience fewer constraints, while single women with no children have no constraints on them in this area.
Chapter: 3. Spatial Interaction and Spatial Behavior
Section: 3.4
AP Topic: 3.6: Contemporary Causes of Diffusion

6. In cases of natural disasters such as floods and earthquakes

    (A) most people tend to resettle elsewhere.

    (B) most people make changes to their homes to make them safer.

    (C) most people tend to come back to their homes in spite of the danger.

    (D) most people migrate as far away as possible from the disaster area.

    (E) most people move away to live with family in other parts of the country.

Answer: C
Feedback: Geographers do not know why, but people do tend to move back to their homes after a disaster. If it is a low incidence occurrence, people tend to think that it will not happen again and their natural optimism makes them think they are safe. Often, they will not modify their homes unless required to do so.
Chapter: 3. Spatial Interaction and Spatial Behavior
Section: 3.5
AP Topic: 1.5: Human Environmental Interaction

7. According to the map showing westward shift of the U.S. population in Figure 3.25 on page 83,

    (A) for the first 50 years, data is not conclusive since the United States did not conduct a census.

    (B) westward expansion was slow in the first 100 years because methods of transportation were poor.

    (C) westward expansion sped up between 1890 and 1950.

    (D) the admission of Alaska and Hawaii to statehood in the 1950s caused a large shift to the west.

    (E) population growth in the Sunbelt had no effect on westward expansion because of a correspondingly large amount of immigration to the East Coast.

Answer: D
Feedback: Since the founding of its Constitution, the United States has conducted censuses to reapportion delegates in the House of Representatives. Movement west was rapid for the first 100 years then slowed from 1890 to 1950. With the advent of air-conditioning, people began to move to the Sunbelt in large numbers, but the biggest change in the 1960 census was the admission of Alaska and Hawaii to statehood, which added many to the population.
Chapter: 3. Spatial Interaction and Spatial Behavior
Section: 3.5
AP Topic: 2.10 Causes of Migration

8. The millions of Soviet citizens who were required by their government to move from rural areas to cities for factory work or from western Russia to labor camps in Siberia are examples of

(A) international migration.

(B) refugees.

(C) forced migration.

(D) pull factors.

(E) guest workers.

Answer: C

Feedback: The example given is intranational (within the same country) migration, not international. The people are not refugees, who are fleeing danger in their homeland. They are also not guest workers, who are invited to come to a foreign country to work. Pull factors are the things that make people want to migrate to another place. At the opposite extreme, the example above shows people who do not want to move but are forced to by their government. Other examples of forced migration would include the Native American Trail of Tears and the slave trade from Africa to the Americas.

Chapter: 3. Spatial Interaction and Spatial Behavior

Section: 3.5

AP Topic: 2.11 Forced and Voluntary Migration

9. Ravenstein's laws of migration state that

(A) most migrants go only a short distance.

(B) most migration proceeds in one long step.

(C) migration is mainly urban to rural areas.

(D) migration only flows one way.

(E) most migrants come into a country illegally.

Answer: A

Feedback: Most migrants go the shortest distance they can from their original homes. Refugees, for example, usually travel into the nearest safe region or across the nearest border only until they feel safe. Most migrants travel in stages, and the majority travel from rural to urban areas. Ravenstein says that, for each migration flow, there is a counterflow, and he says nothing about illegal immigration at all.

Chapter: 3. Spatial Interaction and Spatial Behavior

Section: 3.5

AP Topic: 2.8: Female and Demographic Change

10. An effect of gender on migration is that

(A) women usually decide where the migrating family will go.

(B) studies show that women from countries where they are subservient to men tend to stay subservient even when they move to a country where they have more freedom.

(C) an equal number of men and women migrate.

(D) migrants rarely bring their families with them but prefer to send money home instead.

(E) migration to a developed country gives women fewer economic opportunities and more rights.

Answer: B

Feedback: While more women are beginning to have a say in where their families migrate, most of decisions are still made by men, who usually have more earning power. In the past, men migrated much more often while women stayed home, but today more and more families are migrating either all at once or by chain migration. Migration to a developed country from a more traditional society does bring more economic, social, and political freedom to women, but many are still bound by traditional views and continue to act subserviently to their husbands as they did before.

Chapter: 3. Spatial Interaction and Spatial Behavior

Section: 3.5

AP Topic: 2.8: Female and Demographic Change

Free Response Questions

1. Answer Parts A, B and C below.

(A) Define *external migration* and *internal migration*.

(B) Give examples of external migration and internal migration in North America and South America.

(C) Explain two main causes of migration and give examples of each.

(A) External migration occurs when one leaves his or her own country and moves to another country, while internal migration is movement within the same country.

(B) When someone moves to the United States from Mexico or South America, this is external migration. Internal migration could include old people retiring from the Northern United States to Florida or the Sunbelt.

(C) One of the main causes of migration is to look for better economic opportunities, such as internally someone who moves from the eastern United States to the Pacific Northwest to find a tech job or a person from a rural area of Mexico who leaves his farm to work in a maquiladora on the Mexico-U.S. border. That same person from Mexico might move to the United States to find work in a factory, as a domestic worker or migrant laborer, which is external migration. Another major cause of migration is to escape violence in one's own country or region. People from El Salvador and Guatemala have been traveling in large groups to Mexico and the United States to escape civil unrest that makes their lives unsafe. They hope to claim refugee status.

Rubric: This essay is worth 7 points. One point is given for the definition of internal and external migration. Both definitions must be correct to get this point. Two points are given for the examples in part B. The examples must be from North and South America. Other regions receive no credit. In part C, which is worth 4 points (two for each cause and example) the region is not specified, so from outside the Americas would be acceptable.

Chapter: 3 Spatial Interaction and Spatial Behavior
Section: 3.2
AP Topic: 2.10 Causes of Migration

2. Answer Parts A, B, and C below.

(A) Define *push factors* and *pull factors*.

(B) Explain examples of economic, social, and environmental factors of migration.

(C) Give an example and explain a political barrier to migration.

(A) Push factors are what cause people to want to leave their countries (what is pushing them out), while pull factors are the things that make another country more appealing. As a rule, for each push factor there is a corresponding pull factor.

(B) Economic push and pull factors have to do with the availability of jobs. People leave areas where jobs are not available and move to areas where they are. Social push/pull factors might include religious persecution or intolerance of gay lifestyle. Lack of opportunities for women in some countries, such as Iran, might cause people to leave for more hospitable countries like France. Environmental causes of migration can be natural disasters, such as floods, earthquakes, or tsunamis. After Hurricane Katrina, many people who escaped New Orleans decided to move elsewhere to someplace that was not a flood zone.

(C) A political barrier to migration is something that is put in place by the government to stop migrants from coming in. The United States border fence and the walls built in Israel to keep Palestinians out are two actual physical barriers. Governments can also erect legal barriers, such as quotas like the Chinese Exclusion Act of 1917.

Rubric: This question is worth nine points. The answer receives one point for defining push and pull factors in A, two points each for the economic, social, and environmental examples in B, and two points for the obstacle to migration in C.

Chapter: 3. Spatial Interaction and Spatial Behavior
Section: 3.5
AP Topic: 2.10 Causes of Migration

3. Explain the effects of globalization on retail trade, international banking, transnational corporations, and popular culture.

Globalization, which occurs due to revolutions in communication and transportation, affects every aspect of our lives. Today, instead of going to a brick and mortar store, one can simply pick up a smart phone and order goods from all over the world. A consumer can order clothes from Lands' End or a book from Amazon and have it shipped anywhere in the world. This is causing some actual stores to go out of business, but others can harness the new technology and transportation to make more money than before. Many people own stocks in companies from other countries or invest in monetary funds overseas. International banking and stock trading is done at split-second speed over computers and communications satellites, which means that an international incident will affect the economies of countries all over the world. The attack on the United States on 9/11 affected stock markets worldwide as did the tsunami in Fukushima, Japan. Transnational corporations have offices in several countries and often outsource work to developing countries. Since much of the corporate level work can be done over telephones and computers, executives do not even have to immigrate for work. However, much of the actual manufacturing jobs are located in developing countries where costs are lower, which leads to exploitation of workers and a huge disparity between management and workers' pay. Globalization of culture is easy to see in the ubiquitous nature of clothing around the globe with teenagers wearing jeans and T-shirts with American company logos and businessmen everywhere wearing suits and ties. This Western style dress has taken the place of more traditional clothing styles in many developing countries.

Rubric: This essay is worth eight points, two for each of the effects of globalization. Care must be taken to be specific about which part of the question is being answered since it is not divided into A, B, and C. Label each part that you are answering (transnational corporations, popular culture, etc.)

Chapter: 3. Spatial Interaction and Spatial Behavior
Section: 3.5
AP Topic: 3.6: Contemporary Causes of Diffusion

Population: World Patterns, Regional Trends

AP Introduction

Chapter 4 introduces students to population geography, which deals with the growth, composition, and distribution of people in relation to spatial variations in physical and cultural geographic conditions. Chapter 4 focuses on the second content area of the College Board's AP Human Geography curriculum framework, Unit 2 Population and Migration Patterns and Processes. Chapter 4 addresses the following AP Enduring Understandings from the AP Human Geography course framework:

- Understanding where and how people live is essential to understanding global cultural, political, and economic patterns.
- Changes in population are due to mortality, fertility, and migration, which are influenced by the interplay of environmental, economic, cultural, and political factors.
- Changes in population have long- and short-term effects on a place's economy, culture, and, politics.

AP Concepts and Themes

Chapter Overview

This chapter contains fundamentals of the study of population geography, including the following:
- Influences upon the pattern of human settlement
- The impact of population distribution and density upon society
- Population pyramids to show composition by age and gender
- Population size changes due to fertility and mortality
- Models and theories of population change
- Government policies which encourage or hinder population growth
- Women, gender roles and population change
- Aging populations and social change
- Migration: types, causes, and effects

Learning Objectives

- Identify the factors that influence the distribution of human populations at different scales.
- Define methods geographers use to calculate population density.
- Explain the differences between and the impact of methods used to calculate population density.
- Explain how population distribution and density affect society and the environment.
- Describe elements of population composition used by geographers.
- Explain ways that geographers depict and analyze population composition.
- Explain factors that account for contemporary and historical trends in population growth and decline.
- Explain theories of population growth and decline.
- Explain the intent and effects of various population and immigration policies on population size and composition.
- Explain how the changing role of females has demographic consequences in different parts of the world.
- Explain the causes and consequences of an aging population.

Key Words

Use the terms below with a ▌ to focus your study of AP Human Geography key words in this chapter.

age distribution

▌ age structure

▌ agricultural density

▌ anti-natalist policies

▌ arithmetic density

Boserup thesis

carrying capacity

cohort

▌ crude birth rate (CBR)

▌ crude death rate (CDR)

crude density

demographic equation

demographic momentum

▌ demographic transition

demography

▌ dependency ratio

▌ doubling time

ecumene

Ehrlich, Paul

food security

J-curve

▌ life expectancy

Malthus, Thomas Robert

▌ Malthusian theory

Marx, Karl

▌ migration

▌ mortality rate

neo-Malthusianism

net migration

nonecumene

overpopulation

▌ physiological density

population (demographic) momentum

population density

population distribution

population explosion

population geography

population projection

▌ population pyramid

▌ pro-natalist policies

▌ rate of natural increase

rates

replacement level

S-curve

▌ scale of analysis

Simon, Julian

▌ sex ratio

▌ total fertility rate (TFR)

zero population growth (ZPG)

Note to the Teacher

The following Key Words appear in the AP Course Framework but are not called out as Key Words in the Bjelland Student Edition.

- *Malthusian theory*: the arguments of Thomas Malthus (1760–1834), an English economist. He argued that population grew geometrically whereas food supplies grew only arithmetically, leaving humanity to suffer from famine, disease, and war. More generally, the Malthusian approach argues that there is an upper limit to population size due to a limited carrying capacity of the Earth or local places.

- *natalist policies*: Anti-natalist policies refer to government actions to discourage families from having children. Many countries which are not yet economically developed seek to reduce their birth rate so that societal increases in wealth are not spread across so many people. They may offer information about family planning, subsidize contraception, or publicize the idea that fewer children are better for the family and the country. Pro-natalist policies refer to government actions to encourage families to have children. Many economically developed countries recognize that their total fertility rate, at or below replacement level fertility, needs to increase to avoid societal strain such as a shortage of workers or increasing taxes upon fewer working-age citizens. Governments might subsidize day care, provide a monthly stipend to parents, or simply publicize the need for families to have more children.

- *scale of analysis*: refers to the size of the Earth's surface being considered in any situation. Commonly referenced scales of analysis range from global, regional (e.g. North America), national (i.e. a single country), sub-national (e.g. the Midwest), state, metropolitan, or local. The questions asked by geographers, and the answers arrived at, are dependent upon the scale of analysis.

AP Chapter Discussion and Activities

Identifying Factors Influencing Population Distribution

AP ESSENTIAL KNOWLEDGE: Physical factors, such as climate, land forms, and water bodies, and human factors, including culture, economics, history, and politics, influence the distribution of population.

TEACH: *Tell students to choose a metropolitan area in or near their state and investigate where the population is found within that region. Ask students to consider the following questions: Is the population evenly or unevenly distributed? If unevenly, what influences might have contributed to the pattern observed?*

Remind students that they can use U.S. Census data for various states, counties, or municipalities. An alternate version of this activity is to use a U.S. state or an entire country. Have students share their findings in a class discussion, noting similarities and differences among regions.

Debating the Merits of Larger Populations

AP ESSENTIAL KNOWLEDGE: Population distribution and density affect political, economic, and social processes, including the provision of services such as medical care.

TEACH: *Pose the following question to students: Bigger is often assumed to be better, but is this true when it comes to population? Then conduct a class debate on the merits of larger populations using real-world examples of countries (e.g., China, India, or the United States) or cities (e.g., Shanghai, Mexico City, or London).*

Organize the class into two groups—with one group arguing on the positive aspects of larger populations and the other group arguing on the negative aspects of larger populations. Students should be ready to offer supporting details about how the size or density of a population is an advantage or disadvantage. Encourage students to question one another on their varying viewpoints.

Understanding Uneven Sex Ratios

AP ESSENTIAL KNOWLEDGE: Patterns of age structure and sex ratio vary across different regions and may be mapped and analyzed at different scales.

TEACH: *Remind students that while more male than female babies are born, most societies, communities and places have a roughly 50–50 sex ratio. Ask students what types of places might have very skewed sex ratios, and why?* (Students may offer that cultures in which female children are perceived as a burden or places with high levels of poverty and disease might have skewed sex ratios.) *After a class discussion about general categories of places with uneven sex ratios, have each student research a specific example of a place with an uneven sex ratio. They should consider the following question as they conduct their research: How might the uneven sex ratio shape that place economically, politically, or socially?*

Students can consult the U.S. Bureau of the Census, the Population Reference Bureau, and the World Bank for data and information on the places they are researching. Students should present their findings in a written report that includes maps, charts, or graphs.

Identifying Factors Affecting Fertility Rate

AP ESSENTIAL KNOWLEDGE: Social, cultural, political, and economic factors influence fertility, mortality, and migration rates.

TEACH: *To illustrate how the total fertility rate has changed over time, ask students to research their family tree. The National Archives provides a nice selection of tools and resources to help get started with genealogical research. Tell students they should attempt to go back roughly four generations or approximately 100 years in their research. As they build their family tree, have students consider the following details: How many children were born in each generation? Where was the family living (country, region, or locality)? What year were the children were born? These details will provide context to the number of children born into the family. Ask students to think about how the location of the family and the year the children were born might have influenced how many children were born. What conclusions can students draw from their findings? Have them report their findings in a written report.*

Note that some students may not have access to such family information or do not wish to share such personal information, so an alternate assignment should be made available.

Applying Malthusian Theory

AP ESSENTIAL KNOWLEDGE: Malthusian theory and its critiques are used to analyze population change and its consequences.

TEACH: *Review Thomas Malthus's argument with students.* **Ask:** *What did he believe?* (Malthus argued that human population, if allowed to remain unchecked, would increase at a geometric rate while food supplies would continue to grow at an arithmetic rate. If humans did not limit reproduction, population growth would always outrun the food supply.) *Now remind students that Malthus's argument seems to have been disproven.* **Ask:** *What did Malthus miss in his thinking?* (Malthus did not have the benefit of witnessing advances in medical and agricultural technology.)

Now ask students to consider Malthus's argument as it relates to global climate change (GCC) today. Organize students into two groups to debate Malthus's position in light of GCC and what climate scientists predict will happen over the next 50–100 years. Students in each group should be prepared to defend their positions.

Understanding the Demographic Transition Model

AP ESSENTIAL KNOWLEDGE: The demographic transition model can be used to explain population change over time.

TEACH: *Using Figure 4.16 on page 111, review the stages of the demographic transition model. Have volunteers identify what each line is charting and describe what is happening at various points throughout time. Then have students write summaries that explain what the model is showing. Now discuss with students that while some countries have declining and/or low total fertility rates (TFRs), some countries still have TFRs over five. Ask students to think about why this might be the case, using the demographic transition model as a guide. What factors may be contributing to continuing high TFRs?*

Work with students to select one country to investigate as a case study. Once a specific country is selected, have smaller groups of students research to learn more about the country. Ask students what other statistics seem relevant to explaining the relatively high TFR. Have students discuss their findings as a class.

Examining Population Policies

AP ESSENTIAL KNOWLEDGE: Types of population policies include those that promote or discourage population growth, such as pro-natalist, anti-natalist, and immigration policies.

TEACH: *Discuss with students that national governments often seek to influence the birth rate in their country for varying reasons—some government policies can be pro-natalist, and some can be anti-natalist. Be sure that students fully understand the terms pro-natalist and anti-natalist. Have a class discussion that broadly considers the reasons for pro-natalist and anti-natalist policies.*

Now have students research a specific country that has attempted to influence the birth rate. As they gather information, students should consider the following questions as they pertain to their country of study: Why does the government feel the need to influence the birth rate? How does the government attempt to do so? Is there a cultural, a political, or an economic context to the specific actions of the government that might be different from another country that also has the same pro- or anti-natal policy? Students should present their findings in a written report.

Understanding the Relationship Between the Status of Women and Totally Fertility Rate

AP ESSENTIAL KNOWLEDGE: Changing social, economic, and political roles for females have influenced patterns of fertility, mortality, and migration, as illustrated by Ravenstein's laws of migration.

TEACH: *To explore the association between the status of women and the total fertility rate, have students select a country and compile two types of data. The International Database from the U.S. Census Bureau and the World Bank are great sources for this activity. Students will first obtain the total fertility rate (TFR) for the past 50–100 years for either select years or for each decade of this time space. The second type of data students need to collect for their chosen country, is a list of the years when women gained specific rights.*

After students have completed their research, have them plot the TFR on a graph with the rate on the vertical axis and time on the horizontal axis. Then they should annotate the graph with details of when women gained various rights. Ask students to answer the following questions in one or two paragraphs to accompany their graphs: Do the changes in TFR seem to track with increases in legal, political, economic, or reproductive rights of women? If not, why not?

AP Chapter Feature Answer Key

Geography and Citizenship

1. Essays should reflect an understanding of reproduction and family planning concerns as they exist at a personal level for individuals as well as at a national level as they exist for a government making decisions about population policies. Students should support their positions with evidence from the text or from further research.

2. Answers should include examples of resistance to international concerns over population growth, development, and the environment. Answers should be supported with evidence and should reflect a logical thought process about the question at hand.

3. Presentations should include a logical argument supported with evidence from their research. Students may include visuals such as maps, charts, graphs, photos, or videos in their presentations.

AP Test Practice Answer Key

Below are the Bjelland end-of-chapter AP Test Practice questions along with their answers, feedback, and rubrics.

Multiple Choice Questions

1. Which of the following does NOT strongly impact the birth rate of a country?

   (A) The age and sex structure of its population.

   (B) The customs and family size expectations of its inhabitants.

   (C) The physiological density of the country.

   (D) The population policies of its government.

   (E) The availability of birth control.

   Answer: C
   Feedback: Physiological density is the number of people per farmable (arable) acres of land in a country. Along with population data, this information could help predict a famine, but it does not in itself impact the birth rate of a country. Age and sex structure of a country's population does affect the population since a country made up of many elderly people will not have high population nor will a country that has a severely imbalanced sex ratio. Customs, particularly religious beliefs, affect population growth as do family size expectations. A country's population policy, such as China's One Child Policy or government-provided education and birth control will also lower population growth. At the same time, some countries have tried to raise population growth through government policies to promote having more children.
   Chapter: 4. Population: World Patterns, Regional Trends
   Section: 4.2
   AP Topic: 2.4: Population Dynamics

2. Why is the total fertility rate (TFR) of a country a better measurement of fertility than the crude birth rate (CBR)?

   (A) It shows the average number of children born per woman.

   (B) The TFR, unlike the CBR, is not affected by the age distribution of the population.

   (C) A rate of 2.1 to 2.3 children per woman is considered to be replacement level.

   (D) It is not affected by the child mortality rate.

   (E) They show the difference between high and low fertility countries.

   Answer: B.
   Feedback: The age of the mother does not make a difference in the TFR, so the fact that some countries have more young people or elderly people does not affect it. What matters when looking at the total fertility rate of a country is the number of times during her lifetime a woman will give birth. The child mortality rate does affect TFR, and the replacement levels given in C are correct as is the fact that TFRs let geographers see which countries have high and low fertility, but they do not explain why TFR measures fertility better than CBR. Only answer B does this.
   Chapter: 4. Population: World Patterns, Regional Trends
   Section: 4.2
   AP Topic: 2.4: Population Dynamics

3. Population pyramids such as those shown in Figure 4.9 on page 107 and in Figure 4.12 on page 109 can be used to illustrate all of the following EXCEPT

(A) age and sex distribution patterns of the population.

(B) a comparison of males to females in various age brackets.

(C) the economic problems countries will have if they have too many old people and not enough young people.

(D) the problems of developing countries that have a high dependency ratio.

(E) the reasons for fluctuations during certain years.

Answer: E

Feedback: Population pyramids show the age and sex distributions of an area's population in increments of five years. Males and females at each level can be compared and economic problems can be forecast, such as if an area has too many young people and not enough jobs or too many old people and not enough younger ones to do the work and care for the elderly. High dependency ratios in developing countries mean that they tend to have a lot of young children and not enough older people to care for them. Population pyramids themselves cannot tell geographers WHY there are fluctuations in the numbers of people at certain ages. To understand this, a geographer must know the history of the country. Did it have a terrible famine, an AIDS epidemic, or a war that killed off many people in certain years? These fluctuations will show up on the pyramid. So will reasons for large numbers of men, women, or elderly people in certain areas (an army base, a monastery, or a retirement home).

Chapter: 4. Population: World Patterns, Regional Trends

Section: 4.2

AP Topic: 2.3: Population Composition

4. The changes occurring in the increased rate of the world's population growth and doubling time mean that

(A) the world's population is beginning to shrink and the doubling time is decreasing.

(B) a small increase in the world's population results in a huge increase in numbers even as the doubling time starts to rise.

(C) increases in population in developed countries will continue to offset the decreasing birth rate in developing countries.

(D) when doubling time decreases, world population is growing more slowly.

(E) a J-curve graph of the world's population shows that the population is decreasing.

Answer: B

Feedback: Answer B is correct, and D is wrong. The concept of doubling time means that as doubling time increases, it takes longer for the world's population to double. However, the population is still going up, it is just taking longer for this to happen. This is called demographic momentum. Even a small increase in the world's population will cause it to double eventually. Answer A is incorrect since the world's population is still going up, mainly due to growth in developing countries not in developed countries as seen in Answer C. A J-curve graph does not show a decrease in population but instead shows an increase, so answer E is also incorrect.

Chapter: 4. Population: World Patterns, Regional Trends

Section: 4.2

AP Topic: 2.4: Population Dynamics

5. All of the following are causes for the rapid population growth that began to occur in the mid-18th century EXCEPT

(A) improvements in agriculture and food supply meant fewer famines.

(B) birth rates decreased, allowing for more food and better care.

(C) new medical treatments and technology led to longer life spans.

(D) industrialization and the accompanying urbanization concentrated people into cities where other developments were more available than in rural areas.

(E) improvements in sanitation led to a decrease in death rates.

Answer: B

Feedback: Birth rates did not go down but instead rose in the late 18th and early 19th centuries. Only years after a developing society's culture begins to change are smaller families a result. On the contrary, improved food supply due to changes in agriculture production, new medicines and changes in medical care, availability of new developments due to urbanization, and improvements in sanitation all lead to a lower death rate, which contributes to high population growth.

Chapter: 4. Population: World Patterns, Regional Trends

Section: 4.3

AP Topic: 2.5: The Demographic Transition Model

6. The spread of infectious diseases

(A) has become less frequent over time, resulting in decreased mortality rates.

(B) is affecting fewer people although mortality rates have risen.

(C) began with the Spanish Flu Epidemic of 1918–1919.

(D) is linked to climate change, deforestation, population growth, and urbanization.

(E) can be overcome only by quarantining affected populations.

Answer: D

Feedback: There have been outbreaks of infectious disease throughout history, including the Bubonic Plague outbreak in the 14th century. As people travel more, infectious diseases have spread more often and more rapidly, affecting more people than ever before. There are many ways to stop the spread of infectious diseases, quarantining being only one of them. Improved education, research on disease vectors, clean drinking water, mosquito abatement programs, and many others also help stop disease outbreaks. The only correct answer here is D, that the areas of disease outbreaks are moving due to climate change and deforestation and that population and urban concentrations allow disease to spread more rapidly.

Chapter: 4. Population: World Patterns, Regional Trends

Section: 4.3

AP Topic: 2.5: The Demographic Transition Model

7. The demographic equation means that

(A) the number of people being born is equal to the number of people who die, so population growth is equal to zero.

(B) the final population of an area is equal to the initial population, plus births, minus deaths (rate of natural increase).

(C) the final population of an area is equal to the initial population, plus births, minus deaths, plus the number of migrants coming in and out.

(D) the population growth of an area is rising due to demographic factors.

(E) population growth is declining due to education programs and use of birth control.

Answer: C

Feedback: Answer A is Stage 5 of the demographic transition model. Answer B is not correct because it does not take migration into account. D is a simple statement that has nothing to do with the demographic equation, and although E might be a reason for the result of the demographic equation, only Answer C defines the equation.

Chapter: 4. Population: World Patterns, Regional Trends

Section: 4.4

AP Topic: 2.4: Population Dynamics

8. A major change in family planning, the Cairo Plan for population management in 1994

(A) advocated harsh measures to control population.

(B) was not signed by many United Nations member states because it advocated birth control.

(C) legalized abortion in all United Nations member countries.

(D) targeted education and more rights for women as a way to slow population growth.

(E) was implemented through religious organizations in developing countries.

Answer: D

Feedback: The UN International Conference on Population and Development, which met in Cairo in 1994, was the first such conference to recognize the importance of educating women and granting them a say in their reproductive role. It did not advocate harsh methods to control population, and although it did not mention abortion outright due to many arguments over this issue—particularly with the Catholic Church—it did advocate birth control. It was not implemented through religious organizations. The correct answer, D, is that it advocated using education and the granting of more rights to women, which gave them more reproductive autonomy.

Chapter: 4. Population: World Patterns, Regional Trends

Section: 4.4

AP Topic: 2.7: Population Policies

9. The nonecumene, the very sparsely inhabited or uninhabited parts of the world,

(A) may have localized dense areas of population based on irrigation, agriculture, or mining.

(B) is only found around the polar ice caps.

(C) does not count deserts and high mountaintops where no one could live anyway.

(D) has only been settled by humans in recent years due to advances in technology.

(E) makes up only 10 percent of the Earth's land surface area.

Answer: A

Feedback: The nonecumene, which comprises 35–40 percent of the Earth's land surface area, is made up of the polar ice caps, desert, rainforest, and mountainous areas. They are not totally unpopulated and may have some areas of dense population due to irrigation agriculture or mining. Some of these areas have been settled for thousands of years by people like the Quechua of the Andes mountains.

Chapter: 4. Population: World Patterns, Regional Trends

Section: 4.5

AP Topic: 2.1: Population Distribution

10. Food production will grow arithmetically, and without checks, and that population will grow geometrically, causing people to starve. Where does this idea come from?

(A) It comes from Danish economist Ester Boserup's study of agricultural improvements due to population pressures.

(B) It comes from Thomas Robert Malthus's *An Essay on the Principle of Population.*

(C) It comes from Neo-Malthusians, such as Paul Ehrlich, who wrote *The Population Bomb.*

(D) It was a key belief of communist philosopher Karl Marx.

(E) It was essential to the theories of American economist Julian Simon.

Answer: B

Feedback: Answer B is correct. This sentence basically sums up Malthusian theory. Thomas Robert Malthus, an English economist, wrote his book on population theory in 1798 during the Industrial Revolution in England, beginning the idea that overpopulation might someday become a problem. His ideas did not, of course, consider that birth control methods would be discovered or that new farming methods would be invented, but in the late 1960s, neo-Malthusians, such as Paul Ehrlich, began to sound the alarm again, tying Malthusian theory to other resources along with food supply. Karl Marx's, Ester Boserup's, and Julian Simon's works all attempt to refute Malthus.

Chapter: 4. Population: World Patterns, Regional Trends

Section: 4.7

AP Topic: 2.6: Malthusian Theory

Free Response Questions

1. Choose two of the three countries below and discuss how each of their population policies have changed over the years. What were the results of these policies?

(A) Singapore

(B) China

(C) India

(A) China's One Child Policy, in which people who had more than one child were fined, punished, and sometimes forcibly sterilized, was an extremely harsh method of lowering the birth rate in a totalitarian country. The result of this was a reduced birth rate, but it also resulted in many people killing female babies since males are prized in Chinese culture. The fact that so many male babies were born compared to female babies has resulted in a skewed sex structure with too many young men and not enough women for them to marry.

(B) India's population policy at first relied on government-provided birth control and education, but in the 1970s, a policy of forced sterilization was put into effect. Anger at this policy led to the fall of Indira Gandhi's government, and the new government went back to a policy that emphasized free birth control and education. India's policies have not been as effective as China's, but in a country that is a democracy, the people cannot be forced to do what they do not want or believe in.

(C) Alternatively, the student could write about Singapore, which began a policy to reach negative population growth in the early 1970s. Abortion, birth control, and sterilization were legalized. The government allowed people to have two children but punished those who had more by denying them maternity leave or insurance and by discriminating against their children at school. The result of this policy was an extremely low birth rate, which meant that the government needed to change its policy to get people to have more children through tax incentives. The government also began to take in immigrants from Hong Kong, which brought in more workers who would support their aging population.

Rubric: This essay is worth six points: one for the discussion of each country's population policy, one for the explanation of how it changed, and one for the results. The student should only do two of the countries.

Chapter: 4. Population: World Patterns, Regional Trends

Section: 4.2

AP Topic: 2.7: Population Policies

2. Answer Parts A, B, and C below using the population pyramids for Nigeria and Japan in Figure 4.9 on page 107.

    (A)   Briefly explain the stages of the demographic transition model.

    (B)   Explain the stage of the model Nigeria is in. What is ONE advantage and ONE disadvantage of this stage?

    (C)   Explain the stage of the model Japan is in. What is ONE advantage and ONE disadvantage of this stage?

(A) The demographic transition model is made up of five stages and shows how a country progressed through them. In the first stage, there is a high birth rate and high death rate so that the population of the country remains the same. In the second stage, the death rate begins to decrease but the birth rate remains high, causing the population to rise. By the third stage, the birth rate is starting to go down and the death rate continues to go down as well, so population continues to go up. In the forth stage, the population stabilizes since both the birth and death rates are low. Some countries have reached the fifth stage, in which the birth rate is so low that it is below replacement rate, so the population of the country declines.

(B) Nigeria seems, from the population pyramid, to be in the second stage of the demographic transition mode. There are many births as evidenced by the many young children in the pyramid, but the numbers steadily decline, showing that many of those people are dying at young ages. There are very few old people. A good thing about this is that there are few old people to care for and lots of people working to pay for their care. A bad thing about this is that there are a lot of deaths of young people, so few people live to become elderly.

(C) Japan seems, according to the pyramid, to be in the fifth stage. This means that many people live long lives, so they must have plenty of food, good health care, and an excellent standard of living. The bad thing about being in this stage is that there are fewer and fewer young people to do the work, pay the taxes, and care for the larger and larger number of elderly. A country in this stage is probably going to have trouble paying for its social security and retirement systems.

Explanation: This essay is worth seven points, two for the explanation of the model, one each for knowing which stage Nigeria and Japan are in, one each for the advantages of the stage, and one each for the disadvantages of the stage. Therefore, A = 2, B = 3, and C = 3.

Chapter: 4. Population: World Patterns, Regional Trends

Section: 4.3

AP Topic: 2.5: The Demographic Transition Model

3. Answer Parts A, B, and C using the migration map in Figure 4.20 on page 118.

    (A)   Which is the largest migration stream shown on the map? From where are the migrants coming and to where are they going? Explain ONE economic and ONE social reason for this migration stream.

    (B)   Choose a migration stream that shows a forced migration and explain the reason for it.

    (C)   Explain TWO reasons why people from South Asia migrate to the countries indicated on the map.

(A) The largest migration stream on the map shows people migrating from Western Europe to North America. This stream would have begun in the early 1600s with colonists from France, England, and the Netherlands coming to Quebec, Virginia, and New Amsterdam, respectively. English Puritans and Pilgrims came to Massachusetts to escape religious persecution. Migrants from Europe would continue to arrive in large numbers, pushing the Native Americans off their ancestral lands. With the advent of the Industrial Revolution in the late 1700s and early 1800s, a population explosion in Europe and problems, such as the Irish potato famine and political upheavals in Italy and Germany, saw many more Europeans come to the United States looking to get jobs in factories or to move out West where farmland was still available.

(B) A forced migration would be the stream shown that begins in Africa and leads to Brazil, the Caribbean Islands, and the southern United States. The reason for this migration was that white people wanted laborers for their plantations in the Americas, and African Americans were forcibly captured and transported to work in slavery.

(C) Migrants from countries such as India and Pakistan in South Asia go to the United Kingdom, Australia, and Indonesia. One reason they go to England and Australia is that, since India and Pakistan are former English colonies, many people there already speak English. Going to another place that speaks the same language and where there may be other cultural ties is easier than going to a country in which a different language is spoken. People from India also go to Australia and the United Kingdom because they are more developed countries where better schooling and jobs are available. (A third possible answer is that they go to Indonesia because it is geographically closer and therefore easier to get to.)

Rubric: This essay is worth seven points. In Part A, the students receive one point for recognizing that the largest migration stream goes from Europe to North America. (They must get both the starting place and the ending place correct to get the point.) They receive a second point for an economic reason and a third point for a social reason for migration. In Part B, the students must again name the beginning and ending points of a forced migration to gain one point and explain a reason for it to gain a second point. In Part C, the students will be awarded one point for each of the two reasons given for migration from South Asia.

Chapter: 4. Population: World Patterns, Regional Trends

Section: 4.4

AP Topic: 2.4: Population Dynamics

Language and Religion: Mosaics of Culture

AP Introduction

Chapter 5 introduces students to cultural geography, specifically the topics of language and religion. Chapter 5 focuses on the third content area of the College Board's AP Human Geography curriculum framework, Unit 3 Cultural Patterns and Processes. Chapter 5 addresses the following AP Enduring Understandings from the AP Human Geography course framework:

- Cultural practices vary across geographical locations because of physical geography and available resources.
- The interaction of people contributes to the spread of cultural practices.
- Cultural ideas, practices, and innovations change or disappear over time.

AP Concepts and Themes

Chapter Overview

This chapter contains fundamentals of the study of cultural geography, including the following:

- Language and religion are central components of a culture and thus important influences upon the cultural landscape.
- Language and religion, like other forms of culture, change over time and space.
- Past and present locations of linguistic and religious communities differ because of diffusion from a culture hearth.

Learning Objectives

- Explain patterns and landscapes of language, religion, ethnicity, and gender.
- Explain how historical processes impact current cultural patterns.
- Explain how the process of diffusion results in changes to the cultural landscape.
- Explain what factors lead to the diffusion of universalizing and ethnic religions.

Key Words

Use the terms below with a ▮ to focus your study of AP Human Geography key words in this chapter.

animism	geographic (regional) dialect	monolingual
bilingualism	Hinduism	monotheism
Buddhism	Islam	multilingualism
caste	isogloss	official language
Christianity	Judaism	pidgin
Confucianism	language	polytheism
▮ creole	▮ language family	protolanguage
▮ dialect	▮ lingua franca	religion
▮ ethnic religion	linguistic geography	sacred places

secularism

shamanism

Shinto

speech community

standard language

syncretism

Taoism

‖ toponym

tribal (traditional) religion

‖ universalizing religion

vernacular

AP Chapter Discussion and Activities

Understanding the Diffusion of Language

AP ESSENTIAL KNOWLEDGE: Language families, languages, dialects, world religions, ethnic cultures, and gender roles diffuse from cultural hearths.

TEACH: *To help students recognize that languages often have a common origin, ask them to map basic words in the dominant language of adjacent countries. For example, the Romance languages of French, Spanish, Portuguese, Italian, and Romanian are all derived from Latin. Ask students to pick very basic words such as* water, bread, *or* street *and look them up in each of the Romance languages listed above.*

On an outline map of Europe, have students label the words within each country. Students should be able to see the similarities of the words across the five countries. This will also assist them in thinking about how culture diffuses and how distance from the culture hearth creates chances for local differences in culture. The exercise can be done for other language branches found in a cluster of countries, such as English, Dutch, and German, or Norwegian, Danish, and Swedish.

Comparing Dialects

AP ESSENTIAL KNOWLEDGE: Regional patterns of language, religion, and ethnicity contribute to a sense of place, enhance placemaking, and shape the global cultural landscape.

TEACH: *Remind students that a dialect presents an opportunity to ask questions about why language in one area differs in word choice or pronunciation from another area when both areas speak the same parent language. Discuss the following questions as a class: For the area where your school is located, in what dialect region are you? What words or pronunciations distinguish your dialect area from adjacent dialect areas? Is it possible to map your dialect to see where the transition zone to the next dialect is found? What conclusions can you make about the factors that influenced the culture of your dialect area?*

As an alternative activity, students could choose an area other than their own location and conduct research about the selected location's dialect area using the questions above to guide them.

Understanding How Religion Creates a Sense of Place

AP ESSENTIAL KNOWLEDGE: Religions have distinct places of origin from which they diffused to other locations through different processes. Practices and belief systems impacted how widespread the religion diffused.

TEACH: *Tell students that maps of dominant religions drawn at the global, regional, or even national scales can, depending on how the data is organized, obscure important differences in the practice of those faiths. Explain that some of the most interesting patterns show where different branches or denominations of a faith are found.*

Ask students to select a religious faith with millions of followers who are spatially concentrated—such as Christianity, Islam, or Buddhism—and then create a map showing where the various branches, denominations, or varieties of the selected faith are locally prominent. The purpose of this activity is for students to realize that the fragmentation of Christianity into Orthodox, Catholic, and Protestant branches often coincides with national (state) borders. The same is true with Islam and the Sunni/Shi'ite split. The internal dynamics within a faith are just as meaningful as tensions between adjacent faiths in shaping space and creating place. Depending on the faith selected and the available data, the maps could be drawn at the national, sub-national, or local scale. Once students map the data, ask them to reflect on how the pattern or patterns they find help create a sense of place.

Identifying Spatial Patterns of Ethnic Religions

AP ESSENTIAL KNOWLEDGE: Acculturation, assimilation, syncretism, and multiculturalism are effects of the diffusion of culture

TEACH: *Explain to students that ethnic religions do not seek to gain followers through conversion, instead its members are born into the faith community. This concentrates membership in the faith community near its place of origin and creates a hearth. If these statements are true, then why are ethnic religions practiced outside the hearth area?*

Ask students to select an ethnic religion such as Judaism, Indian Hinduism, or Japanese Shinto and research its spatial pattern at the global scale. Students should consider the following questions to help guide their research: Where outside the hearth are significant numbers of followers of the faith located? Why are they found outside the hearth? Each of the clusters outside the hearth area may have an individual explanation that differs slightly from other clusters of the same faith. Remind students to think about how the processes of acculturation, assimilation, syncretism, and multiculturalism may play a part in the spatial patterns of ethnic religions.

This activity offers a chance for students to review concepts concerning migration found in Chapter 3 on spatial interaction. Drawing upon knowledge of modern world history will also be helpful. Students can complete the assignment by assembling their findings in a written report or a poster.

AP Chapter Feature Answer Key

Geography and Citizenship

1. Students' answers will vary. Encourage students to use local media sources to learn more about the public facilities in your city that have sold their naming rights. If there are no local facilities that have sold naming rights, students should research public facilities in other towns and cities in your state. Students' essays should include correct grammar, spelling, and punctuation, as well as supporting evidence to effectively argue their position on the issue.

2. Students' answers will vary but students should be able to provide thoughtful, logical reasons.

3. Students' presentations should be thoughtfully constructed to provide clear and complete thinking and evidence to support their position.

AP Test Practice Answer Key

Below are the Bjelland end-of-chapter AP Test Practice questions along with their answers, feedback, and rubrics.

Multiple Choice Questions

1. The fact that the nearly 8 billion people on earth speak many thousands of languages

    (A) contributes to the sense of place in different areas and shapes the global cultural landscape.

    (B) explains why there have been numerous wars throughout human history.

    (C) makes it almost impossible for concepts to become globally accepted.

    (D) has led the majority of people to learn English.

    (E) contributes to the homogenization of culture around the world, especially in Africa.

    Answer: A
    Feedback: The idea of "sense of place" is that some things make a place special and different from other places. Diversity in language and religion does this. Different languages are not usually the cause of war, although they may cause some miscommunication. There are many globally accepted concepts, as evidenced by votes in the United Nations on the definition of war crimes, and most people in the world do not learn English—they speak Chinese. And finally, the world's culture is not homogenous, particularly as it pertains to language, and especially in Africa, which numbers over 2,100 languages and language variants.
    Chapter: 5: Language and Religions: Mosaics of Culture
    Section: 5.1
    AP Topic: 3.2: Cultural Landscapes

2. All of the following are true of the Indo-European protolanguage EXCEPT that

(A) it includes both the Romance and Germanic branches.

(B) it is the largest language cluster in the world, spoken by about half of the world's population.

(C) it originated somewhere in Eastern Europe, the Ukrainian steppes, or possibly central Turkey.

(D) its people never managed to get across the Hindu Kush mountains into India.

(E) it does not include Native American or African languages.

Answer: D
Feedback: Indo-European languages include Romance and Germanic languages as well as the languages of India, since its original speakers lived in eastern Europe, the Ukraine or Turkey and migrated to Europe and across the mountains to India. The languages of Native Americans and Africans developed separately from other protolanguages. Indo-European is the largest language cluster.
Chapter: 5: Language and Religions: Mosaics of Culture
Section: 5.1
AP Topic: 3.2 Cultural Landscapes

3. The fact that people in France wear *les blue jeans* and listen to music by *les rappeurs*, and people in Germany practice *das Bodybuilding* and use *der Computer* is evidence of

(A) the development of similar words for things in different languages at the same time.

(B) the spread of English as the lingua franca.

(C) language transfer by relocation diffusion.

(D) the modification of words from a less dominant language.

(E) the takeover of the languages of developing countries by those of developed countries.

Answer: B
Feedback: A is incorrect. These words do not come from different languages. B is the correct answer. English is the language used all over the world in business, science, computers, entertainment, and diplomacy. It is the lingua franca of our age, and English words find their way into other languages due to its spread. This does not occur through relocation diffusion since English speakers are not migrating in great numbers, and these examples use only developed countries, so C, D, and E are not correct.
Chapter: 5: Language and Religions: Mosaics of Culture
Section: 5.1
AP Topic: 3.5: Historical Causes of Diffusion

4. Different dialects of a language

(A) often use different words for the same thing, such as saying "pop" or "soda" when ordering a carbonated beverage, but do not include differences in rhythm and speed.

(B) never coexist in the same geographic space.

(C) are often taught in school and used in government documents instead of the standard version of the language.

(D) are often spoken by people who are bilingual.

(E) include differences in vocabulary, pronunciation, rhythm, and speed.

Answer: E
Feedback: Regional variations in language called *dialects* often use different words for the same thing, like calling a large road a *highway* or a *freeway*, but it also includes the pronunciation of words and the rhythm and speed of speaking. People in the southern United States tend to speak more slowly than do northerners. Different dialects can coexist in the same space, as evidenced by the speaking styles in different areas of London, but usually the standard style of a language is taught in schools and used in official government documents. Bilingualism is a separate issue, meaning that a person speaks more than one language, not more than one dialect of a single language. So, letter E is correct—dialects include the differences in actual words used but also different pronunciation, rhythm, and speed of speaking.
Chapter: 5: Language and Religions: Mosaics of Culture
Section: 5.1
AP Topic: 3.3: Cultural Patterns

5. A pidgin language develops into a creole language when

(A) it becomes the first language of a group of people who have lost their native language.

(B) it becomes more simplified and is only used for certain work-related tasks.

(C) it is adopted by only small isolated groups of people within a country.

(D) it is used by multilingual groups of people to communicate in a third language.

(E) it develops a less complicated vocabulary in which people can express simple ideas.

Answer: A

Feedback: A pidgin language develops when two or more groups that speak different languages develop a simpler language that is a hybrid to communicate with one another in certain circumstances requiring specific work-related vocabulary. When that language comes to be accepted as the first language of the country and becomes more complex with vocabulary that can be used to express more complicated ideas, it has become a creole language.

Chapter: 5: Language and Religions: Mosaics of Culture

Section: 5.1

AP Topic: 3.5: Causes of Historical Diffusion

6. Believers in religious fundamentalism adhere to all of the following EXCEPT the idea that

(A) there are many possible ways of worship that are correct.

(B) correct beliefs are manifested in a specific, sacred text.

(C) traditional cultural and social values must be regained and publicly institutionalized.

(D) secular tendencies of modernity must be rejected since they are a threat to religious beliefs.

(E) they must counteract the cultural changes that undermine religious faith and traditional religious values.

Answer: A

Feedback: Religious fundamentalism is an offshoot of many religions. It consists of groups of people who adhere strictly to traditional, usually scripturally based religious beliefs. They believe that modern society's modern and secular tendencies are wrong, some would even say dangerous. A few groups have even gone so far as to attack symbols of modern secular society, such as the World Trade Center bombing on September 11, 2001, to try to regain traditional values and culture. Religious fundamentalists believe that their religion is the only true faith and that others are incorrect. Therefore, the correct answer to this question is A.

Chapter: 5: Language and Religions: Mosaics of Culture

Section: 5.5

AP Topic: 3.7: Diffusion of Religion and Language

7. Ethnic and tribal (traditional) religions differ from universalizing religions in that

(A) one becomes a member of an ethnic or tribal religion simply by making a declaration of faith.

(B) ethnic and tribal religions do not tend to be associated with a specific territory.

(C) tribal religious beliefs are often closely tied to nature and include shamanism and animism.

(D) ethnic and tribal religions send out missionaries to convert others.

(E) the members of ethnic religions do not form a closed community or associate themselves with a specific ethnic group or political community.

Answer: C

Feedback: Members of universalizing religions such as Islam, Buddhism, and Christianity believe that anyone in the world can join their religion, so while they have a hearth, they are not associated with a specific territory. They often send out missionaries to convert others, and they sometimes use conquest and war to spread their beliefs. Ethnic and tribal religions, on the other hand, are closely associated with specific cultural groups of people in specific areas of land.

Chapter: 5: Language and Religions: Mosaics of Culture

Section: 5.2

AP Topic: 3.7: Diffusion of Religion and Language

8. Study the map in Figure 5.18 on page 154. Which of the following is true about the spatial distribution of religions?

(A) The main religion of Central and South America is animism.

(B) The majority of Protestants live in the eastern United States and Australia.

(C) Hinduism is found on every continent.

(D) Western Europe is mainly Muslim due to the large number of immigrants.

(E) The majority of people in China are Buddhist.

Answer: B

Feedback: Answer B is correct. The majority of people living in the southeastern United States are Southern Baptists while the majority of people in Australia are Church of England, both of which are sects of Protestant Christianity. The main religion of Central and South America is Roman Catholic due to their Spanish heritage. Animists are mainly found in the region of sub-Saharan Africa, Russia, and the Himalayas, while the only place a majority are Hindus is India. Western Europe has had many Muslim immigrants in recent years but not enough to change the majority religion from either Catholic or Protestant Christianity. The majority of people in China do not practice any religion, but those who do practice a combination of Taoism, Buddhism, and Confucianism.

9. The spread of Islam can be attributed to all of the following EXCEPT

(A) relocation diffusion as Muslims have migrated to Indonesia, southern Africa, and the Americas.

(B) expansion diffusion throughout the Arabian Peninsula, North Africa, and northern India.

(C) refugees moving into Western Europe in the late 20th and 21st centuries.

(D) the belief that anyone can become a Muslim if they follow the Five Pillars of Islam.

(E) the Reconquest of Spain in 1492.

Answer: E

Feedback: From Islam's hearth in Mecca, Arabia, the religion spread through the tribal people there and through conquest across North Africa and into India. In the 8th century, the spread of Islam was halted, but Spain stayed a Muslim country until Ferdinand and Isabella led the Reconquest and threw the Muslims out of Spain. They then reinstituted Christianity as the only legal religion. Islam continued to expand in Southern Africa, Indonesia, and the Americas as Muslims migrated to those areas and took their religion with them. The universalizing belief that anyone can become a Muslim is important to the religion's spread.

Chapter: 5: Language and Religions: Mosaics of Culture
Section: 5.6
AP Topic: 3.7: Diffusion of Religion and Language

10. Study the photo of the Ka'ba in Figure 5.25 on page 162 and the photo of the Ganges River in Figure 5.28 on page 164. These images are similar in that they both depict

(A) rituals of a universalizing religion.

(B) major geographic elements of the faith.

(C) pilgrimage sites that are seen as sacred spaces.

(D) actions taken by only a few members of the faith.

(E) the funeral traditions of Islam and Hinduism.

Answer: C

Feedback: Both the Ka'ba, which is the most important sacred place in Islam, and the Ganges River in Varanasi, India, which is one of the seven most sacred places in Hinduism, are places of pilgrimage for their respective religions. The Pilgrimage to Mecca is one of the Five Pillars of Islam, which must be accomplished by every Muslim at least once in his or her life, if possible. Hindus believe that to wash in the sacred rivers aids in rebirth at a higher level and that to die in Varanasi means the end of rebirth. Answer A is incorrect since Hinduism is not a universalizing religion, and B is incorrect because the Ka'ba is not a geographic element like the Ganges River is. Answer D is incorrect since many members of the religions take part in these rituals, and E is wrong since these are not funerary traditions.

Chapter: 5: Language and Religions: Mosaics of Culture
Section: 5.6
AP Topic: 3.3: Cultural Patterns

Free Response Questions

1. Answer Parts A, B, and C below.

(A) Define the word *toponym* and give an example based on the geography, history, or culture of an area.

(B) Explain and give an example of how a toponym can be reflective of the political culture of a time period.

(C) Give two instances in which the toponym of a place has changed and explain why this happened.

A toponym is simply the name of a place (like London or Washington, D.C.), but the naming of places is not a simple matter. Sometimes places are named after the physical geography of a place such as Round Hill, but often Native American words become place names like the Potomac or Shenandoah. Toponyms are often reflective of the politics of a time, such as when a new school or building is named after a politician. Ronald Reagan National Airport in Washington, D.C., or George Bush Intercontinental Airport in Houston, Texas, are good examples. Toponyms are sometimes changed, either when the politics of a time change or when the previous name is later determined to be politically incorrect. The mountain that Native Americans had called *Denali* for centuries was changed to Mt. McKinley after the president was assassinated, but it was changed back in 2015 due to petitions from the Alaskan people. Sometimes place names use terms that were acceptable in their time but are now determined to be racist or sexist, or they were named by conquering peoples. Bombay, India, for example, was named by the British who controlled India until it declared its independence in 1947. Now the Indian people have changed the name to Mumbai.

Rubric: This question is worth eight points. Two points are received for Part A, one for the definition of the word *toponym* and one for the example, which must come physical or cultural geography. Part B is worth two points, for the example of a politically motivated geographic place name and its explanation. Part C is worth four points, two each for the example and explanation of a changing toponym.
Chapter: 5 Language and Religions: Mosaics of Culture
Section: 5.3
AP Topic: 3.7: Diffusion of Religion and Language

2. Answer Parts A, B, and C below.

(A) Give an example and explain the process by which one language is replaced by another.

(B) Give an example in which, instead of taking over, two or more languages came to coexist within one country.

(C) Give an example of a place in which a dying language has been revived and explain two ways this has been accomplished.

(A) One language can come to be replaced by another in several ways. One way is by relocation diffusion. When enough people who speak a different language migrate into an area, particularly if they can take over politically as well, the official language of the area changes. For example, when the British began to colonize Australia and make it a territory of their empire, the languages of the native Aboriginal people were overtaken by English, and many were wiped out altogether.

(B) In some places two languages coexist, such as in Canada. Quebec was originally a French colony, but it became British territory in the 18th century. The Quebecois kept their language but new colonists, who moved farther west, spoke English.

(C) In many places languages that were in danger of dying out have been revived. Welsh, for example, is now being taught in schools again and there is a Welsh language TV station. In Quebec, French has been designated the official language, and laws requiring the use of French have been passed by the regional government.

Rubric: This essay is worth eight points, two each for Parts A and B, and four for Part C. In Part A, an example and explanation of one language taking over from another is required, each gaining one point. In Part B, the student must give an example of a place in which two languages are used to gain the first point and explain how that happened for the second. For Part C, each example and explanation of a way that language can be preserved gains a point.
Chapter: 5 Language and Religions: Mosaics of Culture
Section: 5.1
AP Topic: 3.7: Diffusion of Religion and Language

3. Answer Parts A, B, and C using examples from Europe, the Middle East, or Asia.

(A) Explain one way in which the culture of a place is affected by the religion.

(B) Explain two ways in which religious use of space affects the cultural landscape.

(C) Explain why and give one example of how religious change has caused political or cultural problems to arise.

(A) One way that the religion of a place affects the cultural landscape is in the clothing that people wear. In many Middle Eastern countries, like Saudi Arabia or Iran, women are required to modestly cover themselves by wearing a burka. In Rome, Italy, one sees monks and nuns in their habits everywhere.

(B) Religious beliefs about the use of space affect the cultural landscape of a place in many ways. The first thing that many people notice about an area is its religious architecture. In European countries like France, for example, Catholic church spires can be seen from miles away, dominating the landscape of many towns, while in Muslim countries such as Saudi Arabia the minarets of mosques make obvious what the dominant religion is in that area. Another way that religion affects the use of space is by its requirements for treatment of the dead. In European countries, because of the traditional Christian belief that the dead should be buried, cemeteries take up a lot of land. In Iran, Zoroastrians believe that the dead should be left out in the elements, and they therefore build towers to put the bodies on.

(C) Religious change can cause problems to arise when a group of people of a different religion migrates into an area and the cultural landscape begins to change. Many Muslims, most recently Syrian immigrants, have migrated into Germany, Greece, and Italy in Western Europe in recent years, bringing their religious culture along with them. Some open ethnic restaurants and shops, dress in traditional clothing, and want to build mosques with minarets, all of which angers some Europeans who see the cultural landscape of their towns changing.

Rubric: This essay is worth eight points, two for Part A, two for each of the two examples/explanations in Part B, and one for the example and explanation in Part C. Notice that all the examples given are from the three regions specified in the question. Specific countries are not required, but it is always a good idea to use specific examples, if possible.
Chapter: 5 Language and Religions: Mosaics of Culture
Sections: 5.4 and 5.6
AP Topic: 3.2: Cultural Landscapes

Ethnic Geography: Threads of Diversity

AP Introduction

Chapter 6 introduces students to cultural geography, specifically the topic of ethnicity. Chapter 6 focuses on the third content area of the College Board's AP Human Geography curriculum framework, Unit 3 Cultural Patterns and Processes. Chapter 6 addresses the following AP Enduring Understandings from the AP Human Geography course framework:

- Cultural practices vary across geographical locations because of physical geography and available resources.
- The interaction of people contributes to the spread of cultural practices.
- Cultural ideas, practices, and innovations change or disappear over time.

AP Concepts and Themes

Chapter Overview

This chapter contains fundamentals of the study of cultural geography, including the following:
- Culture traits, including ethnicity, vary across space
- The cultural landscape is the visible imprint of culture upon the surface of the Earth
- Patterns of culture traits, such as ethnicity, help to create place
- Diffusion of cultures can lead to culture change through acculturation and assimilation

Learning Objectives

- Define the characteristics, attitudes, and traits that influence geographers when they study culture.
- Describe the characteristics of cultural landscapes.
- Explain how landscape features and land and resource use reflect cultural beliefs and identities.
- Explain patterns and landscapes of language, religion, ethnicity, and gender.
- Explain how the process of diffusion results in changes to the cultural landscape.
- Explain what factors lead to the diffusion of universalizing and ethnic religions.

Key Words

Use the terms below with a ▮ to focus your study of AP Human Geography key words in this chapter.

▮ acculturation	colony	ethnic island
amalgamation theory	culture rebound	ethnicity
▮ assimilation	ethnic cleansing	ethnic province
chain migration	ethnic enclave	ethnoburb
charter group	ethnic geography	▮ ethnocentrism
cluster migration	ethnic group	first effective settlement

ghetto

host society

natural selection

race

residential dissimilarity index

segregation

social distance

spatial assimilation

tipping point

transnationalism

xenophobia

AP Chapter Discussion and Activities

Identifying Patterns of Culture

AP ESSENTIAL KNOWLEDGE: Colonialism, imperialism, and trade helped to shape patterns and practices of culture.

TEACH: *Explain to students that while smaller areas within the eastern side of both the United States and Canada could be considered to have the English and French respectively as the charter groups, this is not necessarily true for other parts of both countries. On a simple outline map of North America that shows state, provincial, and territorial boundaries, work with the class to draw in some general indication of what culture group might be considered the charter group in the various parts of North America. For each charter group, discuss the rough time period when that group first settled in a particular area. Ask students to describe the patterns and trends they see in the marked-up map.*

Researching Spatial Patterns of Ethnicity

AP ESSENTIAL KNOWLEDGE: Regional patterns of language, religion, and ethnicity contribute to a sense of place, enhance placemaking, and shape the global cultural landscape.

TEACH: *Ask students to select a metropolitan area or a small city in your state or region that has an ethnically diverse population and conduct research to answer the following questions: Where within the metropolitan area or city do various ethnic minorities live? Would you characterize the place where an ethnic minority lives as an ethnic enclave, ethnoburb, or ghetto? If there is more than one ethnic minority in the selected study area, is there a difference in the degree of spatial assimilation and social distance between each of the several ethnic minorities and the dominant culture group? Have students present their findings in a written report that includes maps to help present the information spatially.*

Understanding the Formation of Cultural Landscapes

AP ESSENTIAL KNOWLEDGE: Acculturation, assimilation, syncretism, and multiculturalism are effects of the diffusion of culture.

TEACH: *Help students consider the time element in the formation of a cultural landscape. Explain that some ethnic groups in the United States and Canada have been residents for many decades, if not a century or more. Other ethnic groups are much more recent arrivals.*

For an ethnic group in a city or town near your own, have students determine when that ethnic group first began to establish a presence there. They should consider the following questions, completing outside research if needed: Does this ethnic group show signs of acculturation or assimilation? What characteristics of the ethnic group, the dominant culture, and the locality might have influenced the degree to which the culture of the ethnic group and the dominant culture have changed? Encourage students to discuss their findings with the class.

Inferring Reasons for Cultural Change

AP ESSENTIAL KNOWLEDGE: Cultural ideas and practices are socially constructed and change through both small-scale and large-scale processes such as urbanization and globalization. These processes come to bear on culture through media, technological change, politics, economics, and social relationships.

TEACH: *Remind students that there are a handful of regions within both the United States and Canada that can be characterized as ethnic provinces, but there are not that many when considering the large amount of territory of North America. Ask students to draw upon their knowledge of the history of both countries and consider why are there so few ethnic provinces. Then encourage students to look at this question from a* different angle: Will the few ethnic provinces that exist today likely remain ethnic provinces in 25, 50, or 100 years? If not, what changes in society will transform the cultures of present-day ethnic provinces? Have students write a brief essay that answers these questions.

Drawing Conclusions About Ethnic Diversity and Separatism

AP ESSENTIAL KNOWLEDGE: Regional patterns of language, religion, and ethnicity contribute to a sense of place, enhance placemaking, and shape the global cultural landscape.

TEACH: *Tell students that in many parts of the world with considerable ethnic diversity, separatist movements exist that seek either autonomy or outright sovereignty. Indeed, the community of states have seen a few new members over the last few decades as Eritrea, Timor L'Este, South Sudan, and Montenegro have gained sovereignty. However, not all places which have ethnic diversity have separatist movements or at least separatist movements with considerable public support.*

Ask students to think about countries with considerable ethnic diversity as they create a two-column chart. In one column of the chart, students should list states with no active separatist movements and the other column should include states with active separatist movements. Challenge students to list roughly ten countries in each column. Students should try to include states from multiple world regions to aid in the construction of their mental maps.

After students have completed their charts, have them do a written analysis of their lists, using the examples as the basis for the analysis. They should consider the following questions: Why do some states have considerable ethnic diversity but no significant separatist movement? Why do ethnically diverse states with active separatist movements have this challenge to the state? Students might be interested to include the United States in this activity as there is a separatist movement in Hawaii. They can read ahead in Chapter 12 about political geography to learn about centripetal and centrifugal forces.

AP Chapter Feature Answer Key

Geography and Citizenship

1. Students' answers will vary. Essays should reflect an understanding of the issue and include evidence to support students' positions.

2. Presentations should reflect an understanding of the issue at hand and should include research-based evidence to support one's position. Encourage students to discuss varying opinions as each student shares his or her presentation with the class.

AP Test Practice Answer Key

Below are the Bjelland end-of-chapter AP Test Practice questions along with their answers, feedback, and rubrics.

Multiple Choice Questions

1. The term *ethnicity* signifies

   (A) the categorization of people according to their outward appearance.

   (B) a group of people that all come from the same country.

   (C) people who live together in a specific region or part of a city.

   (D) people who share common culture traits or characteristics.

   (E) a biological definition of humanity based on genetic drift.

   Answer: D

   Feedback: Ethnicity has to do with the culture a person identifies with, not physical characteristics, outward appearance, or genetics. Many different ethnicities can live together in a part of a city, region, or country. While the concept of race affects many people because others may judge them based on their outward appearance, in human geography we are more interested in studying the concept of ethnic identity.

2. According to the graph in Figure 6.4 on page 179,

(A) immigration from South and East Europe peaked between 1900 and 1920.

(B) the largest number of immigrants have always been from Latin America and the Caribbean.

(C) people from Canada never immigrate to the United States.

(D) World War II caused a spike in immigration as Europeans fled the war for safety.

(E) immigration from Africa and Asia are almost equal in number.

Answer: A

Feedback: The graph shows a peak in immigration from South and East Europe between 1900 and 1920. B is incorrect since the places where the largest number of immigrants come from vary over time. The graph shows that some Canadians, although not many, do immigrate to the United States, and there was very little immigration from anywhere during World War II, so C and D are wrong. It also shows that immigration from Asia is significantly higher than immigration from Africa, so E is incorrect as well.

Chapter: 6: Ethnic Geography: Threads of Diversity
Section: 6.2
AP Topic: 3.3 Cultural Patterns

3. The process of acculturation occurs when

(A) the culture of the host country is changed by an influx of immigrants.

(B) immigrant culture is seen as inferior to that of the host country.

(C) there are so many streams of immigrants coming into a country that there is no longer a majority culture.

(D) immigrants begin to adopt aspects of the host country's culture.

(E) immigrants are forced to learn aspects of the host country's culture in order to remain in the country.

Answer: D

Feedback: While host countries are changed by immigrant cultures, as seen in the entry of new words into a language or ethnic neighborhoods and restaurants appearing, the definition of *acculturation* is the adoption of aspects of the host culture by immigrants. This is a process that makes it easier for the immigrant to live in a new land, such as learning the host country's language, but it can also mean that the immigrant loses some aspects of his or her own culture and becomes "assimilated" into the host country's culture.

Chapter: 6: Ethnic Geography: Threads of Diversity
Section: 6.3
AP Topic: 3.8 Effects of Diffusion

4. Ethnic diversity in Yugoslavia and Afghanistan has led to

(A) the integration of various ethnicities within each country into one national identity through the process of assimilation.

(B) the requirement in each country that all people learn a national language.

(C) territorial seizure, war, and ethnic cleansing as various ethnic groups vie for dominance.

(D) support for a national government led by NATO or the United Nations.

(E) the unification of those countries as people put aside their ethnic differences and learned to work together.

Answer: C

Feedback: In Yugoslavia after World War II, Josip Broz was able to hold the many ethnicities together to form a state. After his death, however, fighting between ethnic groups tore the country apart and resulted in attempts by majority groups to exterminate ethnic minorities. Religious differences were a major part of the conflict in Yugoslavia, as they also were in Afghanistan, which has a Sunni Muslim majority and a Shi'ite Muslim minority. There, rivalries between various ethnic groups and warlords, many different spoken languages, and rebels against the central government complicated the situation. The main issue, however, was the existence of many ethnic groups within one country. The correct answer is C. Assimilation did not happen, and there was no thought of a national government led by NATO or the UN. Yugoslavia did not unite. It broke apart into separate states of Serbia, Croatia, Bosnia and Herzegovina, and several others. Fighting is still in progress in Afghanistan as the national government attempts to defeat rebels in several provinces.

Chapter: 6: Ethnic Geography: Threads of Diversity
Section: 6.3
AP Topics: 3.3 Cultural Patterns and 4.8 Defining Devolutionary Factors

5. Examples of ethnic islands and provinces include all of the following EXCEPT

(A) Ukrainians in the Western Prairie provinces of Canada.

(B) Mennonites, Hutterites, and the Pennsylvania Dutch in Canada and the United States.

(C) French Canadians in Quebec.

(D) Native Americans on reservations in the southwestern United States.

(E) Chinatown in San Francisco and other similar enclaves in U.S. cities.

Answer: E

Feedback: The concept of ethnic islands and provinces is a specifically rural one. Answers A and B are both groups of people who came to Canada and the United States to farm and set up rural farming communities. Native Americans in the desert Southwest also live mainly in small rural communities and on scattered farms on reservations. While French Canadians in Quebec live in cities, they also live in small towns and in rural areas. Answer E is the one that does not fit the definition of an ethnic island or province because, although it is about a specific ethnicity, it is urban, not rural in nature.

Chapter: 6: Ethnic Geography: Threads of Diversity
Section: 6.3
AP Topic: 3.3 Cultural Patterns

6. According to the ethnic population maps in Figures 6.13 and 6.14 on pages 190–191, both African American and Hispanic populations

(A) cluster in large cities.

(B) have not migrated in large numbers to North and South Dakota.

(C) are most numerous in the Northeast.

(D) make up 20 percent of the populations of Hawaii and Alaska.

(E) live in the Southwest in large numbers.

Answer: B

Feedback: According to the information provided on the maps, most African Americans tend to live in the southeastern United States while Hispanic Americans tend to live in the southwestern United States. This is mostly due to migration patterns. When enslaved African Americans were brought to America, they were clustered in the South, but they began to migrate north after the Civil War. Hispanic Americans are clustered in the areas of the United States that originally belonged to Spain and that are closer to Mexico, Central America, and South America. Due to the concept of distance decay, there will be more Hispanic Americans and African Americans close to their hearth than there will be farther away from it. Therefore, Answer B is correct. Few African Americans and Hispanic Americans have migrated as far as the upper Midwest.

Chapter: 6: Ethnic Geography: Threads of Diversity
Section: 6.3
AP Topic: 3.6: Contemporary Causes of Diffusion

7. All of the following have influenced the immigration of Asians to the United States EXCEPT

(A) the passage of the Immigration Act of 1965, which abolished earlier limits on immigration that were based on national quotas.

(B) professional preference categories that favored educated Asian immigrants.

(C) the process of chain migration by which legal immigrants could bring their family members to the United States.

(D) the wave of Southeast Asian refugees that came to the United States under the Refugee Resettlement Program after the Vietnam War.

(E) a flood of immigrants from Japan after World War II and from North Korea today.

Answer: E

Feedback: Beginning in the mid-19th century, many Asians came to America to work on the railroads. They opened laundries and Chinese restaurants in California, and after Hawaii was settled, they were brought in to work on sugar and pineapple plantations. Xenophobia and jingoism combined to bring about a wave of anti-immigrant feeling that culminated in the Chinese Exclusion Act of 1917 and other laws that placed limits on immigration. Anti-Japanese sentiments during and after World War II strengthened these feelings and led to the passage of more national quotas. This policy was ended in 1965 with the passage of the Immigration Act, which based entry into the United States on family reunification and set up professional preference categories. Chain migration meant that immigrants already in the United States could bring in their relatives. Many more immigrants came to America as refugees from the Vietnam War. All of the above have contributed to the immigration of Asians to the United States except Answer E. Immigrants from Japan did not flood to America after World War II, and North Korea does not allow people to leave the country.

Chapter: 6: Ethnic Geography: Threads of Diversity
Section: 6.3
AP Topic: 3.6: Contemporary Causes of Diffusion

8. In cities, members of ethnic groups tend to

(A) cluster together with other members of their own group.

(B) disperse evenly throughout the city.

(C) try to assimilate quickly into the majority culture.

(D) move to rural areas where land is less expensive.

(E) join together into multiethnic groups.

Answer: A

Feedback: It is natural for human beings to want to be with people like themselves. New immigrants usually stay near their port of entry and try to find others like themselves. They cluster in neighborhoods where they can speak their language, shop in ethnic grocery stores for products that remind them of home, and go to churches with other members of their community. They do not tend to join with other, different ethnic groups or disperse evenly throughout the city, and they tend to stay in cities where more jobs are available. Ethnic clustering in the past was, and to some extent still is, due to the practice of segregation.

Chapter: 6: Ethnic Geography: Threads of Diversity

Section: 6.4

AP Topic: 3.8: Effects of Diffusion

9. The conversion of an Orthodox Jewish synagogue into a Christian church

(A) shows the importance of the Jewish community in that area.

(B) demonstrates the dominance of Christianity in that area.

(C) is an example of the effect of shifting ethnic concentrations on the cultural landscape.

(D) will cause the migration of more Christians to that area.

(E) is evidence that Orthodox Jews tend to move to more rural areas.

Answer: C

Feedback: While earlier groups of immigrants are moving out of inner cities and into the suburbs, new waves of immigrants are moving in to take their place. These new immigrants are not always from the same place as the older ones, and so the cultural landscape begins to change. An Asian grocery store takes the place of a bodega, or a Latino market moves into what was once Little Italy. Answers A, B, and E are all simply incorrect, while D is an effect, not a cause. The immigration happens first, causing the cultural landscape to change.

Chapter: 6: Ethnic Geography: Threads of Diversity

Section: 6.4

AP Topic: 3.7: Diffusion of Religion and Language

10. In many parts of the United States, Hispanic Americans are no longer a minority group but are instead the majority of the population. This has led to which of the following:

(A) The official language of New Mexico has changed to Spanish.

(B) Recently more immigrants have moved to farms to work as agricultural laborers.

(C) The urban landscape has changed, including colorful murals, advertising in Spanish, and many vendors selling Hispanic food and other goods.

(D) Catholicism has been replaced by Lutheranism as the majority religion.

(E) In recent years, there has been less dispersion and more clustering in cities of specific groups near their point of entry into the United States.

Answer: C

Feedback: The United States has no official language, although in the desert Southwest and other places with high Hispanic American concentrations, many signs, government forms, and other written works exist in both English and Spanish. Hispanic Americans traditionally came into the United States and tended to cluster near their point of entry (e.g. Cubans in Miami and Puerto Ricans in New York City) or near their relatives (chain migration). However more recently, due to the dispersal of large numbers of Hispanic Americans throughout the country, new immigrants have not clustered as much in one place. It was also traditional that Hispanic Americans worked as agricultural workers or *braceros* in many places, but this is less true today. It is untrue that Lutheranism has replaced Catholicism as the majority religion in places with high Hispanic American concentration. What is true is that the urban landscape has changed with signs in Spanish, numerous ethnic restaurants, colorful murals, and grocery stores selling specialties from Central and South America and the Caribbean.

Chapter: 6: Ethnic Geography: Threads of Diversity

Section: 6.3

AP Topic: 3.8: Effects of Diffusion

Free Response Questions

1. Choose three subgroups of Hispanic Americans from the list in Figure 6.6 on page 190. Explain the push and pull factors involved in their immigration to the United States.

   Many Spanish-speaking immigrants have come to the United States from Central and South America and the Caribbean islands. These Hispanic people have different cultures and different reasons for coming to the United States. Mexican Americans often come to the United States in search of work. Traditionally many came to do seasonal, agricultural labor, but today many come to find other kinds of jobs that are not seasonal in nature. The poor economy and lack of job opportunities push them out of Mexico, while the availability of jobs pulls them into the United States.

   They also come to the United States because of proximity. It is the closest developed country and has a long border with Mexico. Cubans began to come to the United States in large numbers after Fidel Castro took over the country in 1959 and instituted a communist regime there. Many were refugees, fleeing danger and oppression in Cuba for the freedom and safety of the United States. Again, proximity was another important reason for choosing the United States. They arrived in Florida since that is the closest part of the United States to Cuba. People from Puerto Rico have come to the United States to look for work and have settled mainly in New York City and New Jersey, looking for jobs. Hurricanes decimate the island regularly and, since Puerto Ricans are American citizens, it is easy for them to immigrate to the mainland.

   Rubric: This answer is worth six points, two each for the explanation of push and pull factors for each of three groups of Hispanic Americans.
   Chapter: 6: Ethnic Geography: Threads of Diversity
   Section: 6.3
   AP Topics: 2.10 Causes of Migration and 3.2 Cultural Landscapes

2. Answer Parts A, B, and C below.

   (A) Define the term *segregation* and explain how it is tied to the idea of social distance.

   (B) Explain the concepts of external and internal controls on spatial patterns within cities, giving two examples of each.

   (C) Explain the concept of shifting concentrations, using a specific example from a city in the United States.

   (A) Social distance is the amount of space between the neighborhoods of different minority groups and the charter group (the original group that was already there). Segregation is the lack of uniform distribution between a minority group and the majority or charter population. Things that cause social distance and segregation are called controls and there are both external ones and internal ones.

   (B) External controls come from outside the minority group. They are things the charter group does to keep the minority group out of their neighborhood or confined to a specific area of a city. This could include unfair housing practices like red-lining, threats, and vandalism. The KKK burning a cross on an African American family's lawn is a good example of an external control. If enough members of a minority group succeed in moving into an area, the charter group will begin to move out, reaching a tipping point, and the neighborhood will change. Internal controls on social distance come from within the minority group itself and include defensive, supportive, and preservationist reasons for the ethnic group to cluster together. Jewish ghettos in European cities existed until the 20th century in some countries and are an example of a defensive ethnic neighborhood. The walls protected people from unfriendly neighbors. Ghettoes also provided support to Jews living there since kosher food and synagogues would be available to the community. Living together in a ghetto also preserved Jewish culture and kept them from becoming too assimilated into European life.

   (C) The concept of shifting concentrations is that neighborhoods change over time as new minority groups come in and old ones move out. Neighborhoods that used to be one specific minority group, such as Little Italy in New York City or Chinatown in San Francisco, become more ethnically mixed. As new waves of immigrants come into the United States, a neighborhood that used to be mainly Irish in the 19th century, for example, might become predominantly Asian in the 1980s and mostly Latino in the 2000s.

   Rubric: This essay is worth seven points. It receives one point for the definition of segregation and social distance. Note that both terms need to be defined to gain ONE point. Students get TWO points for each of the examples used in Part B, for a total of FOUR points, and TWO points for Part C.
   Chapter: 6: Ethnic Geography: Threads of Diversity
   Section: 6.4
   AP Topics: 3.2 Cultural Landscapes and 3.8 Effects of Diffusion

3. Answer Parts A, B, and C below.

   (A) Explain the concepts of cultural transfer and cultural rebound. Give an example of how one of these concepts affects the cultural landscape of a place.

   (B) Describe two examples of American landscapes affected by the culture of either Europe or Latin America.

   (C) Explain and give two examples of ethnic regionalism in Europe.

   (A) Cultural transfer is the idea that when immigrants come to a new country, they will adopt some of the new country's culture, and some of the culture from their old country will affect their new land, as well. Some immigrants assimilate a lot while others try to keep their former ways of life alive. Sometimes people who have lost their original culture "rebound" and become interested in it again. African Americans, who lost much of their culture due to the forced migration of slavery, may wear kente cloth and celebrate Kwanzaa as a symbol of their ancestors' African culture.

(B) Some places in the United States have kept the culture of people who immigrated there long ago. The Pennsylvania Dutch, for example, have managed to keep their culture alive for 200 years, building massive barns, dressing modestly, and using horse-drawn buggies for transportation. Some places use their ethnic heritage to make their land a tourist destination. The Little Switzerland of New Glarus, Wisconsin, and Danish heritage of Solvang, California, are two examples.

(C) Ethnic regionalism, the differentiation of areas of land due to the influence of its people's ethnicity, is still easy to see in many areas of Europe. Slavic communities south of the Danube River have a specific kind of house, called a "smoking room house," which has a covered entrance hall, living area, and stables all under one roof. In Croatia, one story houses are painted blue and have roofs of straw, while Slovenes in the Danube Basin area make their homes of wood and straw-mud.

Rubric: This question is worth eight points. In Part A, one point is given for each of the definitions of cultural transfer and culture rebound. Part B is worth four points, receiving two points each for the two examples of American landscapes affected by the culture of Europe or Latin America. Part C is worth two points, one for each of the examples of regional culture.

Chapter: 6: Ethnic Geography: Threads of Diversity

Sections: 6.5 and 6.6

AP Topic: 3.8: Effects of Diffusion

Cultural Identities and Cultural Landscapes: Diversity and Uniformity

AP Introduction

Chapter 7 introduces students to cultural geography, specifically the topic of ethnicity. Chapter 7 focuses on the third content area of the College Board's AP Human Geography curriculum framework, Unit 3 Cultural Patterns and Processes. Chapter 7 addresses the following AP Enduring Understandings from the AP Human Geography course framework:

- Cultural practices vary across geographical locations because of physical geography and available resources.
- The interaction of people contributes to the spread of cultural practices.
- Cultural ideas, practices, and innovations change or disappear over time.

AP Concepts and Themes

Chapter Overview

This chapter contains fundamentals of the study of cultural geography, including the following:
- Culture traits, including architecture, vary across space
- The cultural landscape is the visible imprint of culture upon the surface of the Earth
- Culture changes through processes such as urbanization and globalization

Learning Objectives

- Define the characteristics, attitudes, and traits that influence geographers when they study culture.
- Describe the characteristics of cultural landscapes.
- Explain how landscape features and land and resource use reflect cultural beliefs and identities.
- Explain how the process of diffusion results in changes to the cultural landscape.
- Explain how historical processes impact current cultural patterns.

Key Words

Use the terms below with a ▌ to focus your study of AP Human Geography key words in this chapter.

▌ culture hearth	material culture	popular region
▌ cultural landscape	metes-and-bounds	Public Land Survey System (PLSS)
custom	neolocalism	rectangular survey
folk culture	New Urbanism	▌ sequential occupation
geodemographic analysis	nonmaterial culture	themed landscapes
glocalization	palimpsest	vernacular house
heritage landscapes	placelessness	vernacular region
long-lot system	popular culture	

AP Chapter Discussion and Activities

Understanding the Impact of Popular Culture

AP ESSENTIAL KNOWLEDGE: Communication technologies, such as the internet and the time-space convergence, are reshaping and accelerating interactions among people; changing cultural practices, as in the increasing use of English and the loss of indigenous languages; and creating cultural convergence and divergence.

TEACH: *Discuss with students that the United States as an economically developed country is very much influenced by popular culture. It is the home of many iconic elements of popular culture, including fast food restaurants and shopping malls. Ask students to think about the following questions: Given the pervasive nature of popular culture in the United States, is everything the same throughout the country or has local difference modified popular culture through neolocalism?*

Then have students survey their community, metropolitan area, or even their home state for evidence and examples that popular culture is not truly uniform in its presence. Students can share the results of their research in written or oral form.

Defining Culture Traits

AP ESSENTIAL KNOWLEDGE: Cultural traits include such things as food preferences, architecture, and land use.

TEACH: *Tell students that the American cultural landscape is very much influenced by the dominant form of transportation: the private automobile. The availability of the car allowed communities to grow and expand outward and for separate residential areas to exist apart from other land uses like industry and commerce.*

Review the concept of New Urbanism with students. Explain that New Urbanism is a land use planning and architecture movement that aims to make neighborhoods more livable by increasing population density, providing a mix of business and residential land uses, and reducing the influence of automobiles. New Urbanism limits urban sprawl by reducing the need for more development at the edge of a community and seeks to make neighborhoods pedestrian-friendly.

Then ask them to evaluate their community or surrounding communities for evidence that the New Urbanism philosophy of land use planning is present. Students might first search the media for reports of real estate projects influenced by New Urbanism and follow up any leads with on-site visits ("ground truthing"). Students should take photos of the neighborhoods they visit for use in a short presentation to the rest of the class.

Extend this activity with a class discussion on how land use is a culture trait and how different land uses shape the overall culture of a place.

Describing Patterns of Sequent Occupance

AP ESSENTIAL KNOWLEDGE: Cultural landscapes are combinations of physical features, agricultural and industrial practices, religious and linguistic characteristics, evidence of sequent occupancy, and other expressions of culture, including traditional and postmodern architecture and land-use patterns.

TEACH: *Remind students that sequent occupance is the succession of cultures that inhabit a place over time. Each culture group creates a cultural landscape that leaves evidence of that group's presence in the form of building styles, toponyms, and field patterns, just to name a few.*

Ask students to look for evidence of sequent occupance in the local community. This could be an immigrant community that clustered in a town or neighborhood of a large city, then after a generation or two assimilated into the dominant group and moved elsewhere, and then was replaced by a new immigrant population. Sequent occupance could also be seen in the gradual replacement of an indigenous society by people from colonial societies as happened in much of the Western Hemisphere.

Students can combine on-site visits with review of area maps to produce an oral presentation containing photographs and maps that demonstrate the succession of culture groups.

Defining Glocalization

AP ESSENTIAL KNOWLEDGE: Acculturation, assimilation, syncretism, and multiculturalism are effects of the diffusion of culture.

TEACH: *Discuss with students that while globalization tends to homogenize culture in places that are economically developed and well-integrated in the global economy, local preference acts to modify forms of popular culture. This is known as glocalization, the local adaptation of the globalization process.*

Direct students to identify aspects of popular culture that they believe to have become globally widespread. This could be forms of music, clothing items like jeans, or the use of social media. How is the element of popular culture modified in multiple places? Tell students to find evidence of glocalization of a single culture trait in five different locations, preferably drawn from multiple regions of the world. Students should be prepared to explain in class what the culture trait is, how it is adapted in the five locations chosen, and what the adaptations indicate about culture change as a process.

Categorizing Elements of Folk Culture

AP ESSENTIAL KNOWLEDGE: Culture comprises the shared practices, technologies, attitudes, and behaviors transmitted by a society.

TEACH: *Explain to students that in the United States, the Amish are a well-known example of a folk culture. Their lifestyle is dramatically different than most Americans, even compared to other rural farming communities. But what if there was a group of people who were less distinct and not widely considered to be a folk culture? How could it be determined if the group was a folk culture or not?*

Ask students to create a series of questions that they believe would, when considered collectively, allow for recognition of folk cultures in any part of the world. The number of questions is not finite but most likely would need to be between five and ten to allow for some degree of certainty. Students should be encouraged to think of questions that would be equally useful in identifying folk cultures in both economically developed and economically developing cultures. Encourage students to share their questions in a class discussion.

AP Chapter Feature Answer Key

Geography and Citizenship

1. Students' answers will vary but should include specific details about one or more of the memorials and civic spaces in their community. Presentations should reflect a deeper knowledge of one local memorial or civic space and include visuals such as images, maps, or videos.

2. Students' essays will vary but should demonstrate an understanding of both sides of this issue, as well as evidence to support their position.

AP Test Practice Answer Key

Below are the Bjelland end-of-chapter AP Test Practice questions along with their answers, feedback, and rubrics.

Multiple Choice Questions

1. Which of the following is true about folk cultures in the United States?

   (A) Folk cultures no longer exist in the United States, having all been supplanted by popular culture.

   (B) Folk cultures only exist among the Amish in Pennsylvania.

   (C) Folk cultures only exist in geographically isolated, rural groups.

   (D) Folk cultures today can only be seen in museums and recreations of the past.

   (E) Folk cultures are inflexible and never adapt to modernity.

Answer: C

Feedback: Folk cultures do still exist in the United States, mainly in geographically or socially isolated groups, such as the Amish and some Native Americans. Folk cultures are showcased in museums and recreations, but that is not the only place they exist. Folk cultures in the United States and elsewhere do adapt to the more modern cultures around them. There are very few untouched folk cultures in the world today.

Chapter: 7 Cultural Identities and Cultural Landscapes: Diversity and Uniformity
Section: 7.1
AP Topic: 3.3 Cultural Patterns

2. All of the following are examples of the persistence of folk culture in advanced society EXCEPT

(A) the popularity of folk music and folk festivals in the United States.

(B) the wearing of kimonos for special occasions in Japan.

(C) the use of chopsticks at restaurants in China.

(D) the adoption of blue jeans and business suits in Kenya.

(E) the prohibition against eating beef in India.

Answer: D

Feedback: Wearing popular style clothing such as business suits and blue jeans is not the traditional style of dress in most developing countries, but it has become the norm. In some countries, traditional dress is still required. Kimonos, chopsticks, and folk music are all parts of folk culture that persist despite the advance of popular culture. As a part of the Hindu religion, the prohibition against eating cows is a part of India's folk culture.

Chapter: 7 Cultural Identities and Cultural Landscapes: Diversity and Uniformity
Section: 7.1
AP Topic: 3.3 Cultural Patterns

3. The culture of the lowland southern United States

(A) is a mixture of French, Irish, and Scottish influences.

(B) mixes English and African elements with traces of French influence from the Mississippi Delta.

(C) is like the northeastern United States due to the influence of French Canadians who migrated there.

(D) includes Native American and Latin American influences from the Spanish colonies in Florida.

(E) is mainly African due to the forced migration of enslaved people to the area in the 18th and 19th centuries.

Answer: B

Feedback: The main cultural influences in the southeastern lowland United States are English, African, and some French. English settlers migrated to the region in the late 17th and 18th centuries. The slave trade brought many Africans and their cultures to the area, and an influx of French settlers to the area around New Orleans added to the mix as well. Scottish and Irish settlers lived further north in the mountains of Tennessee and Kentucky, while Native Americans were forced out of the Southeast in the 1820s. Spanish colonies in Florida had little influence on the rest of the Southeast.

Chapter: 7 Cultural Identities and Cultural Landscapes: Diversity and Uniformity
Section: 7.1
AP Topic: 3.8 Effects of Diffusion

4. Popular culture refers to

(A) the general mass of people, mostly urban and suburban, within a country who are constantly conforming to, changing, and adopting new trends and fads.

(B) the rural farm communities which dictate nationalistic culture to the rest of the nation.

(C) the combination of religion, language, food, housing and other artifacts that influence the lives of a group of people.

(D) the required cultural adoption of totalitarian societies.

(E) the culture found in very small, isolated areas.

Answer: A

Feedback: The definition of popular culture is that it is mainly urban and suburban in nature, homogenous throughout a large area, and quickly changing. Often it is spread through and influenced by the media.

Chapter: 7 Cultural Identities and Cultural Landscapes: Diversity and Uniformity
Section: 7.1
AP Topic: 3.1 Introduction to Culture

5. An example of regionalism in popular culture is that

(A) everyone can watch the same shows on TV.

(B) cricket is a popular sport in England and India.

(C) soccer attracts over 600 million sports fans globally.

(D) Canadian and American cultures are very similar.

(E) McDonalds restaurants are found all over the world.

Answer: B

Feedback: Regionalism in popular culture means that a trend manifests differences in different regions. While cricket is extremely popular in Britain and the former British Empire, it is relatively unknown in other parts of the world. People in various parts of Southeast Asia, for example, wear a long strip of cloth draped in different ways around their bodies—sarongs in Indonesia, saris in India, etc.

Chapter: 7 Cultural Identities and Cultural Landscapes: Diversity and Uniformity

Section: 7.1

AP Topic: 1.7 Regional Analysis

6. The concept of placelessness causes

(A) areas in different regions to look different from one another.

(B) people to protest the arrival of Walmart and McDonalds.

(C) folk culture to resist the takeover by popular culture.

(D) universalizing religions to diffuse to more remote areas.

(E) people to get lost while traveling.

Answer: B

Feedback: The concept of placelessness means that, as popular culture replaces folk culture in an area, local businesses are replaced by chain stores and restaurants, causing the cultural landscape to look the same as many other places. This globalization of culture causes protests by local people against businesses such as Walmart and McDonalds because they drive local shops out of business and cause the area to lose its regional flavor.

Chapter: 7 Cultural Identities and Cultural Landscapes: Diversity and Uniformity

Section: 7.1

AP Topic: 3.2: Cultural Landscapes

7. The concept of glocalization is described as

(A) the takeover of small local businesses by large corporations.

(B) the practice of outsourcing jobs to developing countries where labor is cheaper.

(C) the homogenization of the cultural landscape as all shopping areas begin to look the same.

(D) the practice of universalizing religions of sending missionaries to convert people.

(E) the small changes that are made in a global business to make it popular in a specific locality.

Answer: E

Feedback: Glocalization is when a business makes changes so that it will appeal to local culture. McDonalds, for example, sells kosher Big Macs in Israel and chicken Big Macs in India, where people do not eat beef.

Chapter: 7 Cultural Identities and Cultural Landscapes: Diversity and Uniformity

Section: 7.1

AP Topic: 3.6: Contemporary Causes of Diffusion

8. A reason for the distribution of smokers on the map in Figure 7.16 on page 224 is

(A) in areas where the fewest people watch baseball, many people smoke cigarettes.

(B) in areas where the fewest people watch baseball, very few people smoke as well.

(C) a below average number of people smoke and watch baseball in the same regions.

(D) more people smoke in tobacco-producing regions.

(E) more tobacco is imported into the southeastern United States.

Answer: D

Feedback: In areas where tobacco is produced, more people tend to smoke. Tobacco is exported from, not imported into, the southeastern United States. Although the two maps do show that in areas where fewer people watch baseball, many people smoke, there is no correlation between the two cultural traits.

Chapter: 7 Cultural Identities and Cultural Landscapes: Diversity and Uniformity

Section: 7.1

AP Topic: 3.2: Cultural Landscapes

9. Folk houses tend to be

(A) much alike in many regions of the world since the poorest people live in them.

(B) extremely diverse since they are built of local materials and must deal with local conditions.

(C) built of expensive materials that are imported from far away.

(D) very uncomfortable since they have no heat or air-conditioning.

(E) circular in shape with roofs made of thatch or leaves.

Answer: B

Explanation: Folk houses are very diverse, from round yurts in Mongolia to rectangular sod houses in Iceland. They are made from local materials, rarely brought from far away, and are made to deal with local weather and geographic conditions. Houses in areas with lots of snow have sharply pointed roofs to allow the snow to fall off. Houses in hot areas are built to allow air flow to cool them.

Chapter: 7 Cultural Identities and Cultural Landscapes: Diversity and Uniformity

Section: 7.2

AP Topic: 3.2: Cultural Landscapes

10. The concept of New Urbanism promotes

(A) the movement of people from cities to planned suburban communities.

(B) gentrification as poorer people are unable to afford to stay in newer neighborhoods.

(C) walkability and mixed-use buildings within cities.

(D) the building of large shopping malls and stadiums.

(E) the relocation of young people to small towns.

Answer: C

Feedback: New Urbanism is the idea of building mixed-use residential/office/retail buildings in city neighborhoods. This promotes walkability since people can live, work, and shop in the same place. It also makes the place have a small-town feel and can promote a more diverse-looking landscape. It is not a suburban or a small-town movement, nor does it promote gentrification.

Chapter: 7 Cultural Identities and Cultural Landscapes: Diversity and Uniformity

Section: 7.2

AP Topic: 6.8: Urban Sustainability

Free Response Questions

1. Choose two types of American folk music and explain the following:

(A) the hearth of each musical type

(B) the initial influence on the musical type

(C) the ways in which the music has changed as it diffused

Northeastern style folk music originated in England and diffused to the United States with the original settlers. French influences came down from Canada as well. It is characterized by ballads sung unaccompanied by instruments. Scottish and Irish immigrants brought some change to the music, and often bagpipes or fiddles accompanied dance music. Southern Backwoods and Appalachian style music is also influenced by its British, Irish, and Scottish roots, but the people there were much poorer. The solo singing is very nasal in tone and the subject matter is often very sad due to the hard lives of the people. This music is the hearth of today's country music. These two song traditions merged in the Western style music tradition, which is influenced by the lives of the rivermen and cowboys of the West. Many of the songs take a northern ballad and rework it in a more southern style.

Rubric: This answer is worth eight points, one point for each musical type's hearth in Part A, one point for each type of music's initial influence in Part B, and two points each for explaining the way that each type of music changed as it diffused in Part C.

Chapter: 7 Cultural Identities and Cultural Landscapes: Diversity and Uniformity

Section: 7.1

AP Topic: 3.2: Cultural Landscapes

2. Answer Parts A, B, and C below.

(A) Explain how monuments and memorials contribute to the cultural landscape of a country.

(B) Give one example of a national memorial or monument in the United States and explain how it fits into the cultural landscape.

(C) Explain one way that a memorial or monument can cause division within a country.

Monuments and memorials contribute to the cultural landscape of a country or region by fostering a shared cultural identity among its people. The symbols on the monuments, who is honored by them, and how the past should be remembered are transmitted to successive generations of people through their monuments. A good example of this is the Martin Luther King, Jr., Memorial in Washington, D.C. The honoring of Dr. King, who died for the cause of equality, is something that resonates with all American people, but particularly with African Americans since he was assassinated for fighting for African American rights. One way that a memorial can be divisive is if different people from different regions of a country interpret their history differently. The fight over whether to keep or tear down memorials to Confederate soldiers is a good example of this. Some people in the South see the memorials as a part of their history which should be kept, while others (especially African Americans) see these memorials as honoring those who fought to keep slavery alive.

Rubric: The essay above is worth six points, two for each part of the question.

Chapter: 7 Cultural Identities and Cultural Landscapes: Diversity and Uniformity

Section: 7.2

AP Topics: 3.2: Cultural Landscapes; 4.1: Introduction to Political Geography

3. Look at the images in Figure 7.32 on page 235, Figure 7.37 on page 237, and Figure 7.39 on page 238. Describe the regional housing style, the materials used, and the importance of the style in the cultural landscape for each of the following:

(A)   the Northeast

(B)   Charleston

(C)   the Southwest

Traditional housing styles in the United States are influenced by the climate and materials available in the region, as well as by the culture of the people who originally settled there. In the Northeastern United States, which was settled by English, French, and Dutch people in the 17th century, Dutch colonial homes and English style homes with heavy framed beams are typical. Along the southern coast, houses in cities like Charleston, South Carolina, are turned sideways to catch the cooling coastal breezes. Deep porches block the sun that would otherwise come through the windows and heat up the house. In the desert Southwest, where it is even hotter, houses are often made of adobe with thick walls to block out the heat. This style, originally that of the Native Americans in the region, was adopted by the Spanish who settled there, and it is still used frequently today. All three of these housing styles give their region a totally different look from anywhere else in the country. People travel to Charleston to walk among the live oaks and take in the gentility of the old neighborhoods. Tourists come to the desert Southwest to eat spicy food, buy Native American crafts, and photograph the pueblos. The landscape of each area is unique and special, both geographically and historically.

Rubric: This question is worth nine points, one each for the housing style, the materials used, and the cultural landscape, for each of the three examples.

Chapter: 7 Cultural Identities and Cultural Landscapes: Diversity and Uniformity

Section: 7.2

AP Topic: 3.2: Cultural Landscapes

Economic Geography: Primary Activities

AP Introduction

Chapter 8 introduces students to economic geography, specifically the topic of primary sector activities, including agriculture. Chapter 8 focuses on the fifth content area of the College Board's AP Human Geography curriculum framework, Unit 5 Agriculture and Rural Land-Use Patterns and Processes. Chapter 8 addresses the following AP Enduring Understandings from the AP Human Geography course framework:

- Availability of resources and cultural practices influence agricultural practices and land-use patterns. Agricultural production and consumption patterns vary in different locations, presenting different environmental, social, economic, and cultural opportunities and challenges.
- Agriculture has changed over time because of cultural diffusion and advances in technology.
- Agricultural production and consumption patterns vary in different locations, presenting different environmental, social, economic, and cultural opportunities and challenges.
- Industrialization, past and present, has facilitated improvements in standards of living, but it has also contributed to geographically uneven development.

AP Concepts and Themes

Chapter Overview

This chapter contains fundamentals of the study of economic geography, including the following:

- The physical environment is a significant influence upon the way agriculture is practiced.
- The Green Revolution transformed commercial agriculture.
- Agricultural production regions are partly shaped by land values.
- Commercial farms have grown in complexity of operation as part of commodity markets.
- The von Thünen model of rural land use emphasizes transportation cost to move products to market.
- The global economy includes food and other agricultural products in a supply chain.
- The way in which agriculture is practiced alters the environment, sometimes with significant negative consequences for society.
- Present-day agricultural practices invite critical analysis of their sustainability.
- The role of women in agriculture differs between societies.

Learning Objectives

- Explain the connection between physical geography and agricultural practices.
- Explain the consequences of the Green Revolution on food supply and the environment in the developing world.
- Explain how economic forces influence agricultural practices.
- Describe how the Von Thünen model is used to explain patterns of agricultural production at various scales.
- Explain the interdependence among regions of agricultural production and consumption.
- Explain how agricultural practices have environmental and societal consequences.

- Explain challenges and debates related to the changing nature of contemporary agriculture and food production practices.
- Explain geographic variations in female roles in food production and consumption.
- Explain the spatial patterns of industrial production and development.

Key Words

Use the terms below with a ▌ to focus your study of AP Human Geography key words in this chapter.

agriculture	▌ intensive commercial agriculture	renewable resource
aquaculture	▌ intensive subsistence agriculture	resource
Boserup thesis	market economy	secondary activity
▌ commercial agriculture	▌ market gardening	service activity
commercial economy	maximum sustainable yield	▌ shifting cultivation
▌ commodity chain	Mediterranean agriculture	▌ soil salinization
▌ deforestation	natural resource	▌ subsistence agriculture
▌ desertification	nomadic herding	subsistence economy
economic geography	nonrenewable resource	technology
▌ extensive commercial agriculture	▌ pastoral nomadism	tertiary activity
▌ extensive subsistence agriculture	planned economy	tragedy of the commons
extractive industry	▌ plantation agriculture	truck farm
gathering industry	post-industrial	usable reserves
genetically modified (GM) crops	primary activity	▌ von Thünen model
▌ Green Revolution	quaternary activity	

Note to the Teacher

The term *soil salinization* appears in the AP Course Framework but is not called out as a Key Word in the Bjelland Student Edition. Soil salinization occurs when water evaporates from farm fields. The substitution of irrigation water for precipitation in warm, arid climates results in large amounts of water evaporating from farm fields. The irrigation water, containing a high concentration of dissolved minerals, leaves a mineral crust on top of the soil upon evaporation. Over time increasing concentrations of salt prevent the growth of many types of plants, effectively removing the farm fields from cultivation.

AP Chapter Discussion and Activities

Identifying Categories of Economic Activities

AP ESSENTIAL KNOWLEDGE: The different economic sectors—including primary, secondary, tertiary, quaternary, and quinary—are characterized by distinct development patterns.

TEACH: *To assist students in distinguishing between the types of economic sectors, compile a list of local businesses that students might be familiar with. Work with the class to help students categorize each business as being a primary, secondary, tertiary, or quaternary activity. If you use a sufficiently large number of businesses, roughly 50 or more, ask students to reflect on the relative number of businesses in each of the four sectors.*

Depending on the size and nature of the business community in your area, there is a good chance that most of the businesses will be correctly categorized as tertiary sector. This will help students recognize that the United States has a post-industrial economy where the tertiary or service sector is the core of the economy. You might also discuss with students the areas of the country that have a concentration of other types of primary, secondary, and quaternary businesses.

Explaining the Interdependence of Food Production and Consumption

AP ESSENTIAL KNOWLEDGE: Food and other agricultural products are part of a global supply chain.

TEACH: *Students may have a poor awareness of where their food is produced. To help them have a better understanding, ask them to create a list of basic food categories such as fruits, vegetables, meat and poultry, seafood, dairy, and grains. Then ask students where food items in each of these categories might be produced for sale in your local area.*

Encourage students to determine production areas by visiting grocery stores and asking the managers of various departments in the store from where the food comes. If students have connections to local restaurants, they may be able to ask similar questions of the chefs or people in charge of purchasing. A third option is to contact area food wholesalers that supply local businesses. While some food items may come long distances, such as tropical fruits or fresh fruits and vegetables during the winter, other items might be produced within a one-to-two-hour drive of your community. Ask the students to map the production areas for the several food categories and write up a potential explanation for the patterns they detect. For example, students will likely see that dairy products, because they are perishable, tend to be produced somewhat close to where they are consumed.

Understanding the Relationship Between the Economy and the Environment

AP ESSENTIAL KNOWLEDGE: Environmental effects of agriculture land use include pollution, land cover change, desertification, soil salinization, and conservation efforts.

TEACH: *To help students appreciate the difference between renewable and non-renewable resources, ask students to create a table of 10–20 natural resources they consider important to the proper workings of the national economy. Students should categorize the resources as renewable or non-renewable, noting the approximate amount of time necessary for the resource to be (re)created. The time frame could be a few years in the case of commercially valuable fish species or millions of years in the case of petroleum.*

For those resources considered to be renewable, students should also indicate in the table whether the specific resource has a maximum sustained yield and what that might be. Students should assemble the desired information and create a poster to display the categories and associated information. Lastly, considering the resources chosen, their status as renewable/non-renewable, time frame to generate the resource, and a possible maximum-sustained yield, ask students to write a paragraph inferring how society should manage natural resources.

Drawing Conclusions About the Green Revolution

AP ESSENTIAL KNOWLEDGE: The Green Revolution had positive and negative consequences for both human populations and the environment.

TEACH: *Explain to students that the Green Revolution is deserving of the designation as a "revolution" because crop production was transformed using specially bred crop varieties, machinery, fertilizer, and pesticides. But the Green Revolution is also regarded as a revolution by the increased harvests measured by bushels per acre of farmland.*

To help students realize how much the supply of staple crops increased thanks to the Green Revolution, ask them to research typical yields for three main crops affected by the Green Revolution: corn, wheat, and rice. For each crop, students should determine a typical yield per unit of farmland both before and after the adoption of Green Revolution techniques. Note that figures reported in scientific, agricultural, or government publications might give a range of yields rather than a discrete figure. In addition, the yield and unit of farmland might be given in a metric weight and area instead of bushels and acres.

Have students assemble the data they gather into a table for analysis. Among the questions students might be asked to consider are: Which crop showed the greatest percentage increase in yield? Which parts of the world consume these three crops as a major part of the diet? Were there any negative consequences of the Green Revolution? Students should submit the table along with a written analysis including any additional insights from the data.

Evaluating Von Thünen's Model

AP ESSENTIAL KNOWLEDGE: Von Thünen's model helps to explain rural land use by emphasizing the importance of transportation costs associated with distance from the market; however, regions of specialty farming do not always conform to von Thünen's concentric rings.

TEACH: *Discuss with students that the von Thünen model of agricultural production, like other models, attempts to identify key influences or relationships by simplifying reality. Von Thünen incorporated several assumptions into his model including that there was only a single market, the soil was of uniform quality in all locations, and that there were no physical barriers to transportation, such as a mountain. This allowed him to isolate the key variable of distance from the market, and then to determine what rural land use was most profitable at certain distances from the market.*

To help students improve their understanding of both models in general and von Thünen in particular, ask them to consider what other variables today influence where varieties of agriculture occur. For example, what about the role of government incentives or penalties? What about the local food or farm-to-table movement? Ask students to think broadly and creatively about influences upon the location of food production and to envision additional variables that a present-day von Thünen would have to assume away to focus on distance to market. Use these questions to guide a class discussion.

Determining the Effects of Climate Change on Agriculture

AP ESSENTIAL KNOWLEDGE: Environmental effects of agriculture land use include pollution, land cover change, desertification, soil salinization, and conservation efforts.

TEACH: *Tell students that while humanity can use science and technology to create many advantages for farmers, agriculture is still very much influenced by the natural environment. Global climate change (GCC) is expected to alter long-standing patterns of temperature and rainfall, which will have significant impacts upon agriculture.*

Ask students to investigate GCC to determine the sort of environmental changes scientists predict will occur over the next half century. With that information, how will agriculture be affected? Students should select a region to use as a case study of how GCC will affect agriculture. The following questions should help guide students' research: Which of the expected GCC impacts are expected to be significant to the region of study? Will the changes be beneficial, harmful, or some of both? Will all forms of agriculture be affected or just some? Have students present their findings in a written report.

AP Chapter Feature Answer Key

Geography and Citizenship

1. Students' answers will vary but should reflect an understanding of the issue and be supported with research-based evidence.

2. Students' answers will vary but should include clear reasoning.

3. Students' essays will vary but should include correct grammar, style, and punctuation as well as an understanding of the issue at hand.

AP Test Practice Answer Key

Below are the Bjelland end-of-chapter AP Test Practice questions along with their answers, feedback, and rubrics.

Multiple Choice Questions

1. The processing of cattle into meat products, dog food, and fertilizer is

(A) an example of a primary economic activity that can be done on small family farms or large commercial farms.

(B) a primary activity when done on a farm but secondary if done in a factory.

(C) a part of the Green Revolution that led to higher yield agriculture and fewer famines.

(D) a secondary economic activity often done in large-scale commercial agriculture operations that are replacing family-owned farms.

(E) an economic activity that is declining as more people become vegetarians.

Answer: D

Feedback: While the raising of cattle is a primary economic activity, processing the meat is a secondary activity. Transporting the meat and selling it in a store would be a tertiary activity. In many developed countries, meat production is often done on large commercial farms, which are replacing small family-owned farms.

Chapter: 8: Economic Geography: Primary Activities

Section: 8.1

AP Topic: 7.2: Economic Sectors and Patterns

2. According to the map in Figure 8.7 on page 253, the area of the world in which agriculture makes the largest contribution to the GDP (gross domestic product) is

(A) South America.

(B) Southeast Asia.

(C) North America

(D) Sub-Saharan Africa.

(E) North Africa.

Answer: D

Feedback: As a rule, the least developed countries have the most people participating in agriculture. While developed countries might produce more per farmer due to the use of advanced technology, developing countries have many more farmers practicing subsistence agriculture. They have not moved into manufacturing or the service sector, and therefore the majority of the country's GDP comes from farming.

Chapter: 8: Economic Geography: Primary Activities

Section: 8.2

AP Topic: 7.2 Economic Sectors and Patterns

3. The process of shifting cultivation

(A) is mainly done in tropical areas where large rainfall amounts deplete the soil quickly if it is used for too long.

(B) requires farmers to rotate their crops in two or three fields to avoid soil depletion.

(C) is a way to avoid rainforest destruction in developing countries.

(D) is practiced by a large percentage of the world's population.

(E) has been practiced in developed countries as part of the Green Revolution.

Answer: A

Feedback: The process of shifting cultivation is practiced in tropical developing countries, where heavy rains leach the nutrients out of the soil very quickly. It is only practiced by a small percentage of the world's population. It involves hacking down the vegetation of an area and burning the stubble, then planting crops for a few years before moving on. It is a major cause of deforestation in the rainforest areas where it is practiced.

Chapter: 8: Economic Geography: Primary Activities

Section: 8.2

AP Topic: 5.6 Agricultural Production Regions

4. Rice farming in China and other Asian countries

(A)   is classified as a type of extensive agricultural production because it requires the use of so much land and water.

(B)   can be done on small family farms.

(C)   has required people to alter the landscape to increase food production.

(D)   is practiced as a type of urban subsistence farming.

(E)   has diffused to Europe and the Middle East over the course of the 19th century.

Answer: C

Feedback: Extensive agriculture is practiced on large tracts of land like ranches, often with few people involved. Rice farming is classified as a form of intensive agricultural production since it requires many people and several steps in the production process. Irrigation of fields, transplanting seedlings, draining the fields and harvesting the crop all require a large amount of manual labor. It also requires the alteration of the natural landscape as the people dig irrigation ditches which alternately flood and dry out the area. Because of the necessary climatic conditions and work requirements, rice farming is still mainly done in China and Southeast Asia. It has not diffused to Europe or the Middle East, which do not have a good climate to support rice production. Therefore, the cultures of these areas do not include much rice in their diets.

Chapter: 8: Economic Geography: Primary Activities

Section: 8.2

AP Topic: 5.1 Introduction to Agriculture

5. The participation of women in agricultural production

(A)   has declined due to increased educational opportunities and the movement of women into factory work.

(B)   has increased in developed countries but is very low in developing countries due to religious and cultural prohibitions against women working.

(C)   has had little effect on the lives of families in developing countries.

(D)   is extremely important since women grow over half the world's food supply.

(E)   has declined in those countries that practice intensive forms of agriculture.

Answer: D

Feedback: Women participate in extremely large numbers in agricultural production, especially in developing countries. As men have gone into factory work, women have taken their places in the fields. Women grow 80 percent of the food for their families in developing countries.

Chapter: 8: Economic Geography: Primary Activities

Section: 8.2

AP Topic: 5.12 Women in Agriculture

6. According to the map in Figure 8.12 on page 262, the issue of crop diversity is important because

(A)   many varieties of crops have gone extinct in the past 100 years.

(B)   loss of diversity is particularly bad in the Mediterranean region and India.

(C)   commercial agriculture has allowed more diversity of crops than traditional family farms.

(D)   thousands of species comprise the world's food supply today.

(E)   crop breeders require diversity to breed new varieties of crops that will be resistant to new pests and diseases.

Answer: E

Feedback: Lack of crop diversity is a problem because hundreds of plants have gone extinct in recent years, particularly in rainforest regions. Family farms typically grow more diverse kinds of crops than do commercial farms which tend to specialize in only one species. The problem with lack of diversity is that diseases tend to strike one kind of plant or another. When there is no crop diversity, the chance of a devastating crop disease rises exponentially. In addition, many rainforest plants that we have not tested yet or even discovered may be the cure for diseases.

7. The disadvantages of livestock factory farms include all of the following EXCEPT

(A)   the pollution of streams and groundwater due to mismanagement of animal waste.

(B)   the overuse of antibiotics and vitamins to speed growth and maintain animal health.

(C)   the production of a high volume of animal products for the least possible cost.

(D)   the confinement of animals in small enclosures.

(E)   the takeover of traditional family farms by large agribusiness.

Answer: C

Feedback: The goal of factory farming is to produce a large amount of animal products for the least possible cost and then to sell those products for a profit. This in itself is not a disadvantage, but it can lead to the possible mistreatment of animals and pollution of the environment. Overuse of antibiotics, vitamins, and growth hormones can also be harmful to people if they are in the food that is being consumed. The destruction of family farms is also harmful to the traditional way of life in many countries.

Chapter: 8: Economic Geography: Primary Activities

Section: 8.2

AP Topic: 5.11 Challenges of Contemporary Agriculture

8. Mediterranean agriculture

(A)   is found not only around the Mediterranean Sea but also around the Baltic and Caspian Seas.

(B)   relies heavily on wet, intensive farming methods.

(C)   consists of large plantations that grow cash crops like coffee and sugar.

(D)   is done in conjunction with truck farming to bring produce to small European markets.

(E)   is a specialized form of agriculture known for grapes, olives, oranges, and other fruits and vegetables.

Answer: E

Feedback: Mediterranean agriculture is found in any area with a Mediterranean climate, which includes parts of Europe, the Middle East and North Africa, but it is also practiced in the northwest coastal United States. It involves production of specialized products such as olives, grapes, figs, oranges, and other fruits and vegetables.

Chapter: 8: Economic Geography: Primary Activities

Section: 8.2

AP Topic: 5.6 Agricultural Production Regions

9. Aquaculture refers to

(A)   the culture of coastal areas that revolves around the lives of fishermen and boating.

(B)   commercial deep-sea fishing operations.

(C)   the breeding of fish in freshwater ponds or in fenced-off areas of bays and estuaries.

(D)   raising seaweed and other marine vegetation for human consumption.

(E)   the hunting of marine mammals for their meat and oil products.

Answer: C

Feedback: Aquaculture is the breeding of commercial fish either in freshwater or salt water contained areas.

Chapter: 8: Economic Geography: Primary Activities

Section: 8.3

AP Topic: 5.1 Introduction to Agriculture

10. The cost of production of metallic minerals, such as copper and iron, is influenced by all of the following factors EXCEPT

(A)   the amount of ore available.

(B)   the acceptance of the local population.

(C)   the richness of the resource deposit.

(D)   the distance from the site of the resource to the market.

(E)   land acquisition and royalty costs.

Answer: B

Feedback: The cost of mining a product is influenced by various site and situation factors. A small deposit or one that is not very rich might not be worth the cost of mining it. The distance it must be transported is important since metal ores are heavy. Land acquisition and royalty costs are often high and add to the cost of production. Acceptance of the local population can be problematic when it comes to getting permission to mine, but it does little to affect the cost.

Chapter: 8: Economic Geography: Primary Activities

Section: 8.3

AP Topic: 7.2 Economic Sectors and Patterns

Free Response Questions

1. Answer Parts A, B, and C below.

(A) Define the term *Green Revolution* and explain its importance to agricultural production.

(B) Explain one demographic result and one economic result of the Green Revolution.

(C) Explain two negative consequences of the Green Revolution.

(A) The Green Revolution can be defined as the innovations in agricultural production that began in the 1940s with the invention of new kinds of wheat, which allowed that grain to be grown in drier conditions. These innovations continued with the development of chemical fertilizers, which allowed farmers to intensively cultivate their crops without fear of exhausting the soil, and pesticides and herbicides which raised production immensely.

(B) One demographic result of the Green Revolution is that, because more food can be produced in drier climates, there are fewer famines, leading to more population growth. An economic result is that farmers in areas which had been extremely poor farming regions are now able to export grain and make money instead of being subsistence farmers. Mexico is a good example of this after the introduction of dwarf wheat for which Borlaug won a Nobel Prize.

(C) Two negative consequences of the Green Revolution are pollution and the rise of commercial farming at the expense of small family farms. Pollution is an issue because farmers can overuse fertilizers, pesticides, and herbicides, and when it rains, they wash into nearby waterways, polluting the water and poisoning wildlife and people. The Green Revolution has also caused the rise of commercial farms because pesticides, herbicides, fertilizer, and especially the modified seeds are very expensive. Small farmers often cannot afford them. They cannot compete with the prices of large commercial farms and are driven out of business.

Rubric: This answer is worth seven points. To get one point for Part A, the student must both define and explain. If only one part is done, the point is not awarded. For Part B the student is awarded one point each for the two results of the Green Revolution. The answers must be about demographic and economic results—other types of results will not gain the points even if they are correct. Each of the negative consequences in Part C is worth two points since an explanation is required as well. A student can get one point for naming the negative consequence and the second point for explaining it.

Chapter: 8: Economic Geography: Primary Activities

Section: 8.2

AP Topic: 5.5 The Green Revolution

2. Study the diagram in Figure 8.14 on page 264 to answer Parts A, B, and C below.

(A) Describe the von Thünen model and explain what it is used for.

(B) Explain one of the problems with using the von Thünen model.

(C) Explain how and why the von Thünen model can be modified.

(A) The von Thünen model of agricultural production shows, in concentric rings around a market, where various crops can be grown and still make a profit for the farmer. It specifically considers the cost of transporting various crops, either because of their fragility or difficulty of transport. For example, dairy products and flowers must be grown in the area closest to the market to avoid being spoiled. Forest products were traditionally shown in the second ring from the market because lumber would be heavy to transport. In rings further out, field crops could be grown, and the farthest ring was for ranch land.

(B) One of the problems with using the von Thünen model today is that it was made before modern transportation made it easier to transport farm products. Now in developed countries, we can easily transport flowers from Holland and bananas from South America. Much of American meat and grain production is done in the Midwest, far from the population centers of the east and west coasts, which shows that the von Thünen model does not work when a country has an excellent transportation system. The von Thünen model still works well in developing countries where transportation is less certain and refrigeration is often not available.

(C) Another problem with the von Thünen model is that it does not take geographic features of the area into account. Those features might modify what can be grown in the area or how easily produce can be transported. The model must be modified if a river runs through the area or a rocky hill protrudes. A river causes the rings of the model to elongate along both sides of the river bed because the river can often be used for transportation of farm products from further away. A mountain or hill, on the other hand, causes the rings to distort because it may be a barrier to transporting products, necessitating a costly detour.

Rubric: This question is worth 7 points, one for the description of the von Thunen model, and two for the explanation in Part A. In Part B, the essay receives two points, one for describing a problem with the model and a second point for explaining it. In Part C, the essay receives two points for explaining how the model can be modified.

3. Answer Parts A, B, and C below.

(A) Explain the difference between extensive and intensive subsistence agriculture.

(B) Give one example of extensive subsistence agriculture, explain why it is used, and one advantage or disadvantage of the practice.

(C) Give one example of intensive subsistence agriculture, explain why it is used, and one advantage or disadvantage of the practice.

(A) Extensive subsistence farming involves large areas of land and minimal labor per acre, while intensive subsistence farming involves small areas of land but a lot of work per acre.

(B) An example of extensive subsistence agriculture is nomadic herding, which involves keeping livestock in large areas of unfenced land, allowing them to wander and graze on the natural foods available there. In the dry grasslands of the Asian steppes and in sub-Saharan Africa, people practice nomadic herding because other types of farming will not work there. Animals that can survive in harsh conditions, such as sheep, goats, and camels, are kept for local consumption, not to take to market. To the people who live in these areas, nomadic herding is what keeps them alive. In some places, people practice transhumance, in which they take their animals to higher elevations in the summer and to lower ones in the winter. In this way, they avoid the extreme climate of winter in the high mountains and they also avoid over-grazing the land.

(C) An example of intensive subsistence agriculture is rice farming. The planting of seeds, transferring the seedlings to flooded fields, and then allowing the water to drain off for harvest (which must be done through a complicated system of irrigation) all takes an incredible amount of labor on a small amount of land. Often several crops a year will be planted like this. A disadvantage, aside from the exhausting amount of work needed, is that a large amount of fertilizer is needed to grow several crops a year without depleting the soil. When the water is drained out of fields for harvest, the fertilizer, too, drains away into waterways used for drinking water and eventually into the ocean, which can have an adverse effect on marine life.

Rubric: This essay is worth nine points. In Part A both intensive and extensive agriculture must be explained correctly to gain one point. Part B is worth four points, two for explaining a type of extensive subsistence agriculture and why it is practiced in a specific place, and two for either an advantage or a disadvantage of the practice. Part C is worth four points, two for explaining a type of extensive subsistence agriculture and why it is practiced in a specific place, and two for either an advantage or a disadvantage of the practice.

Chapter: 8: Economic Geography: Primary Activities
Section: 8.2
AP Topic: 5.1 Introduction to Agriculture

Economic Geography: Manufacturing and Services

AP Introduction

Chapter 9 introduces students to economic geography, specifically the topics of manufacturing and services. Chapter 9 focuses on the seventh content area of the College Board's AP Human Geography curriculum framework, Unit 7 Industrial and Economic Development, Patterns and Processes. Chapter 9 addresses the following AP Enduring Understandings from the AP Human Geography course framework:

- Industrialization, past and present, has facilitated improvements in standards of living, but it has also contributed to geographically uneven development.
- Economic and social development happens at different times and rates in different places.
- Environmental problems stemming from industrialization may be remedied through sustainable development strategies.

AP Concepts and Themes

Chapter Overview

This chapter contains fundamentals of the study of economic geography, including the following:

- The secondary sector of economic activity has a distinct spatial pattern.
- Secondary and tertiary sector activities in a global capitalist economy locate where it is most profitable despite international borders.
- Changes in the cost of doing business, as well as government regulations, spur shifts in the geography of manufacturing and services.

Learning Objectives

- Explain how the Industrial Revolution facilitated the growth and diffusion of industrialization.
- Explain the spatial patterns of industrial production and development.
- Describe social and economic measures of development.
- Explain causes and geographic consequences of recent economic changes such as the increase in international trade, deindustrialization, and growing interdependence in the world economy.
- Explain how sustainability principles relate to and impact industrialization and spatial development.

Key Words

Use the terms below with a ▌ to focus your study of AP Human Geography key words in this chapter.

agglomeration

agglomeration economy

▌break-of-bulk point

brownfield

commodity chain

▌comparative advantage

▌complementarity

consumer service

deindustrialization

deglomeration

external economies

footloose

Fordism

foreign direct investment (FDI)

▌free trade agreement

freight rate

▌Industrial Revolution

infrastructure

▌least-cost theory

line-haul cost

locational interdependence

maquiladora

market equilibrium

market orientation

multiplier effect

▌natural resources

new international division of labor (NIDL)

offshoring

▌outsourcing

▌primary activity

producer service

▌quaternary sector

▌quinary sector

satisficing location

▌secondary activity

spatially fixed cost

spatially variable cost

spatial margin of profitability

substitution principle

▌tariff

terminal cost

▌tertiary activity

transnational corporation (TNC)

ubiquitous industry

uniform (isotropic) plain

Weberian analysis

Note to the Teacher

The following Key Words appear in the AP Course Framework but are not called out as Key Words in the Bjelland Student Edition.

- *free trade agreement*: An international economic agreement whereby products made in one member country can be sold in another member country without being charged a tariff.
- *quinary sector*: Some typologies of economic sectors contain a fifth sector. This is essentially a subset of the tertiary (service) sector but focused on very sophisticated decision making, such as scientific research.
- *tariff*: A tax charged on imported products to protect domestic producers of the same items against competing foreign firms with a lower cost basis.

AP Chapter Discussion and Activities

Understanding the Relationship Between Secondary Activities and Infrastructure

AP ESSENTIAL KNOWLEDGE: Labor, transportation (including shipping containers), the break-of-bulk point, least-cost theory, markets, and resources influence the location of manufacturing, such as core, semiperiphery, and periphery locations.

TEACH: *Explain to students that one of the key influences on the spatial behavior of secondary sector firms is the presence of infrastructure, the built structures which facilitate commerce. Examples of infrastructure include expressways, railroads, airports, ports, pipelines, major electrical transmission lines, high speed internet connections, canals, and possibly other examples.*

Ask students to survey the infrastructure of a town, city, or county near where they live. They should consider the following questions as they gather information: What types of infrastructure are present? Are certain companies or industries located in close proximity to that infrastructure, like a trucking company with a depot right off a major highway? Have businesses left or come to the area because of the infrastructure?

Tell students to make a simple sketch map of the area of study, including the infrastructure and noteworthy businesses which might take advantage of the infrastructure. Students should write up an analysis of their map, reflecting on what they found and how it might influence the decision making of company leaders and community development officials.

Identifying Patterns of Economic Activity

AP ESSENTIAL KNOWLEDGE: The different economic sectors—including primary, secondary, tertiary, quaternary, and quinary—are characterized by distinct development patterns.

TEACH: *Review the concept of agglomeration economies. Then tell students that businesses in the same industry often cluster together to take advantage of agglomeration economies. While some of the well-known examples of agglomeration are found in a few key areas (e.g. tech firms in Silicon Valley, California), other examples are found at the local scale throughout North America.*

Ask students to investigate a business district near their home to see what types of businesses are found there and where within the business district these companies operate. Discourage students from using shopping malls and so-called lifestyle centers as they are not good choices to investigate because they typically have a much more restricted range of businesses and represent a single owner who decides which businesses may rent space there.

As students conduct their research, tell them to consider the following: Are there multiple competing businesses, such as a cluster of car dealerships on an "Auto Mile" or several restaurants within a few blocks of each other? Are there concentrations of related businesses? For example, on the "Auto Mile" there are likely other car-related businesses like auto parts stores, repair shops, rental car companies, and car washes.

With the information collected, students should make a simple sketch map, color coding businesses by category to help the clusters (agglomerations) stand out. In addition to the map, have students write a short analysis of what they observed and how they explain the locational decisions of the businesses.

Studying Changes in the Spatial Patterns of Economic Activity

AP ESSENTIAL KNOWLEDGE: Labor, transportation (including shipping containers), the break-of-bulk point, least cost theory, markets, and resources influence the location of manufacturing, such as core, semiperiphery, and periphery locations.

TEACH: *Remind students that spatial patterns change over time, and this is often reflected in the businesses or even entire industries that have left one location for another. Ask students to investigate changes in the business community in their town, county, or part of their state over the past 10–20 years, paying attention to the secondary and tertiary sectors. Students should use the following questions to guide their research: Have businesses outsourced some jobs to another firm? Has a business moved production offshore to take advantage of lower labor costs? Has a transnational corporation shifted its headquarters to another country to take advantage of lower tax rates?*

Students might already know of some prominent examples but could find more information by checking local media archives. Some newspapers have a decade or more of old issues contained within their own websites, while others could be accessed through a library database. Students should share their findings in a written report, explaining what businesses moved, why they moved, and where they moved to. Students should then synthesize the individual examples and make some general statements about business behavior and the local economy.

Understanding Complementarity

AP ESSENTIAL KNOWLEDGE: Complementarity and comparative advantage establish the basis for trade.

TEACH: *Explain to students that complementarity exists when goods available in one location are needed in, affordable to, and able to be transported to another location. Have students think about the goods and services produced in your state or region. Then discuss the following questions: Where do the goods and services produced in your state or region go? This could be to other U.S. states or to other countries. Where do imports coming into your state or region originate from? If needed, encourage students to use online resources to help them answer these questions. Discuss examples of complementarity that emerge.*

Identifying Break-of-Bulk Points

AP ESSENTIAL KNOWLEDGE: Labor, transportation (including shipping containers), the break-of-bulk point, least cost theory, markets, and resources influence the location of manufacturing, such as core, semiperiphery, and periphery locations.

TEACH: *Explain to students that products shipped in large quantities, especially commodities like petroleum, coal, metal ores, grains, and timber, are more efficiently transported by bulk carriers. These include oceangoing ships, large barges on navigable rivers, trains pulling tank or hopper cars, and pipelines. At some point, however, the bulk carrier cannot proceed farther due to a change in the physical geography (e.g., rapids in a river or mountains), the end of a rail line, or the need to distribute the shipment in smaller quantities to the final customer. These break-of-bulk points require transfer to a new form of transportation and are often the site of industrial activity.*

Direct the students to survey the local area for actual and potential break-of-bulk points while considering multiple transportation forms including pipelines, ships, railroads, and highways. Have students create a simple sketch map showing the location of these sites as well as a few landmarks to help orient the map reader. Students should write a description and analysis of the area's break-of-bulk points, using these questions to guide them: Are there any such points that have not been developed, or have been abandoned (e.g., a canal that was filled in or a rail spur that has been converted to a trail)? In light of the region's economy and the available break-of-bulk points, are there types of businesses that could potentially begin to operate there? To extend this activity, discuss break-of-bulk points in places around the world.

Applying Least-Cost Theory

AP ESSENTIAL KNOWLEDGE: Labor, transportation (including shipping containers), the break-of-bulk point, least-cost theory, markets, and resources influence the location of manufacturing, such as core, semiperiphery, and periphery locations.

TEACH: *Tell students that while the United States has largely deindustrialized since the 1960s, there is still industrial activity in the assembly of vehicles, aircraft, construction equipment, and light machinery. The production of some metals, such as steel and aluminum, also still occurs in the United States.*

Ask students to identify a business near the school that can be categorized as a secondary sector activity. Using Weber's least-cost model of industrial location, students should attempt to determine the relative importance to that business of (1) transportation costs, (2) labor costs, and (3) agglomeration costs. Students can consider the nature of the company's activities to estimate the importance (low, medium, high) of each of the three variables. Students should think about whether the business being studied has a market or raw material orientation as well as whether the substitution principle may apply to their business model.

This activity lends itself well to a group activity with students sharing responsibility for obtaining information about the businesses' different types of costs. Have each group make a class presentation to share their findings.

Defining Comparative Advantage

AP ESSENTIAL KNOWLEDGE: Complementarity and comparative advantage establish the basis for trade.

TEACH: *Review with students that the theory of comparative advantage states that each region should specialize in the type of economic activity that it does best. For the region of the state in which you live, have students consider what products or classes of products might be judged to be the region's comparative advantage.*

Students can use these questions to guide their thinking: What is it about the region that gives it a comparative advantage over other parts of North America or other countries in the production of that product? Is the region's comparative advantage likely to remain even as globalization and the trend toward free-trade agreements make competition from other regions more frequent? Moderate a class discussion for students to share their answers.

AP Chapter Feature Answer Key

Geography and Citizenship

1. Students' position papers should provide evidence to support their position. Papers should include correct grammar, style, and punctuation.

2. Presentations should reflect students' understanding of location theory and include succinct arguments to support their position on this issue. Students might include media coverage of a specific example to help support their position. Presentations should include visuals, such as charts, graphs, maps, photos, or videos.

AP Test Practice Answer Key

Below are the Bjelland end-of-chapter AP Test Practice questions along with their answers, feedback, and rubrics.

Multiple Choice Questions

1. The shift from manufacturing jobs to service-oriented jobs, or deindustrialization,

    (A) caused new steel mills to open in Silicon Valley even as the old mills closed in the northeastern United States.

    (B) was caused by the high prices of manufactured goods in developing countries, such as China.

    (C) occurred as many people moved into research and tech related industries.

    (D) was mainly caused by the number of service workers such as maids, secretaries, and janitors.

    (E) caused many service jobs to be outsourced to developing countries where labor is cheaper.

    Answer: C
    Feedback: The shift in the 1980s from manufacturing to service sector jobs caused many factories, including steel mills, in the United States to close. Less expensive manufactured goods could be gotten from developing countries, and highly educated Americans moved into research- and tech-related jobs in places like Silicon Valley, the North Carolina Research Triangle, and the Princeton Corridor. While the number of service workers, such as maids and secretaries, climbed, it was not the cause of the change. Service jobs, such as telemarketing, are sometimes outsourced to developing countries, but again, this is not the cause for the shift from manufacturing to service work.
    Chapter: 9: Economic Geography: Manufacturing and Services
    Sections: 9.1 and 9.4
    AP Topic: 7.2 Economic Sectors and Patterns

2. According to Alfred Weber's least-cost theory, the most important factor in determining the location of an industry is

    (A) the cost of transporting raw materials to the factory and finished products to market.

    (B) the availability and cost of labor.

    (C) the agglomeration of people and productive activities.

    (D) the formation of diseconomies with higher rents and wage levels.

    (E) the amount of political interference or subsidies provided by the government.

    Answer: A
    Feedback: According to Weber, three things are important for determining where a factory should be located—the cost of labor, the cost of transportation, and agglomeration. However, he saw the transportation aspect as being most important for factory location because, when working with heavy or hard-to-transport raw materials, costs can be kept down by locating near the source of the raw materials. If the raw materials are easy to transport but the finished product is more delicate, the factory must be located nearer to the market. A copper smelter, for example, must be located closer to the copper mine so that money is not wasted transporting the tons of rock that bear the ore. A potato chip factory, on the other hand, would be better located near the market since potatoes are easily transportable but once made into chips, they are very fragile.
    Chapter: 9: Economic Geography: Manufacturing and Services
    Section: 9.2
    AP Topic: 7.2 Economic Sectors and Patterns

3. The least expensive mode of long-distance freight hauling is by

   (A) airplane.
   (B) boat.
   (C) truck.
   (D) railroad.
   (E) pipeline.

   Answer: B
   Feedback: Using waterways, either ocean or inland waterways, such as rivers or canals, is the cheapest method of moving large amounts of goods over long distances. While trucking is more flexible geographically than railroads, it uses more fuel and cannot haul as much freight at one time. Pipelines are good for liquids only, and airplanes are best used for moving the consultants and executives of companies who need to get places in a hurry regardless of the cost.
   Chapter: 9: Economic Geography: Manufacturing and Services
   Section: 9.2
   AP Topic: 7.2 Economic Sectors and Patterns

4. Break-of-bulk points are important to the production of manufactured goods because

   (A) they allow governments to assess tariffs on foreign goods coming into the country.
   (B) they are where a factory should be located to minimize the cost of raw materials.
   (C) heavier, more bulky items are harder to transport, so they cost more.
   (D) the change from one type of transportation method to another method changes the cost of the finished product.
   (E) the search for raw materials led to the colonizing of South America, Africa, and Southeast Asia.

   Answer: D
   Feedback: A break-of-bulk point is a place where goods are shifted from one mode of transportation to another, which will always affect the cost one way or another. Shifting to a cheaper mode of transportation, from air to truck for example, would significantly lower costs, while bringing goods into a port on a ship and then switching them to a train would make them cost more. In addition, it is important to note that each time a product is unloaded and then reloaded, there is the additional cost of labor for doing this work.
   Chapter: 9: Economic Geography: Manufacturing and Services
   Section: 9.2
   AP Topic: 7.2 Economic Sectors and Patterns

5. Governments can stimulate industrial development by all the following methods EXCEPT

   (A) building highways and regulating interstate commerce.
   (B) offering incentive programs to bring industry into an area.
   (C) passing lenient land use and zoning laws.
   (D) enforcing strict environmental codes.
   (E) building industrial parks and investing in large development projects.

   Answer: D
   Feedback: Building highways makes transportation of raw materials and finished products easier, which helps industry, as does regulating interstate trade. Many places offer tax breaks, lenient zoning, and other incentives to attract businesses. Building industrial parks and large development projects aids in agglomeration, which is attractive to manufacturing. However, strict enforcement of environmental laws has led many companies to move their factories out of developed countries and into developing countries where they can make their products more cheaply.
   Chapter: 9: Economic Geography: Manufacturing and Services
   Section: 9.2
   AP Topic: 7.8 Sustainable Development

6. The practice of establishing maquiladoras along the Mexican border

   (A) was made illegal by the Mexican government in the 1960s.
   (B) has led to the immigration of many Mexicans, who are searching for better jobs, in the United States.
   (C) allows goods to be made in Mexico at a low cost and then transported to the United States for sale.
   (D) has led to a flood of cheap, badly-made products coming into the United States.
   (E) has hurt the Mexican economy since it takes jobs and money away from Mexican people.

Answer: C

Feedback: A maquiladora is an assembly plant that puts together products to be sold in the United States. Because the work is done in Mexico by workers who get paid less than American workers and because factories do not have to follow the high standards required in American plants, the goods cost less than if they were made in the United States. Maquiladora products are not badly made, and the assembly plants themselves provide work for Mexican people, which helps the economy of their country. It has led many Mexicans to move from other parts of Mexico to the area near the border, but it has not caused them to migrate to the United States.

Chapter: 9: Economic Geography: Manufacturing and Services

Section: 9.2

AP Topic: 7.7 Changes as a Result of the World Economy

7. The main impact of transnational corporations comes from

(A) foreign direct investment in the 50 least-developed countries.

(B) investment in countries that are the farthest away geographically from the parent company.

(C) interdependence in the world economy between the more-developed countries and those that provide raw materials and manufacturing.

(D) shipments of manufactured goods from more-developed countries.

(E) outsourcing of services to call centers.

Answer: C

Feedback: Transnational corporations make foreign direct investments, but very little goes to the least-developed countries. Of the top 100 transnational corporations, 91 are in the United States, Europe, and Japan. They tend to invest in countries that are geographically closer to them, and while they may outsource services to call centers, this is a small part of what they do. The main impact of transnational corporations is that they link the economies of many countries into one global economy, which means that when something happens (good or bad) to one country's economy, it affects all the others.

Chapter: 9: Economic Geography: Manufacturing and Services

Section: 9.2

AP Topic: 7.5 Trade and the World Economy

8. According to the chart in Figure 9.21 on page 307, the largest change in the economic sectors of the economy occurred when

(A) the secondary sector grew between 1850 and 1900 due to the Industrial Revolution.

(B) the number of farmers shrank to only 1 percent in 2010.

(C) the number of agricultural and manufacturing jobs grew at the expense of tertiary work.

(D) the number of people in manufacturing greatly outnumbered farmers in the 1920s.

(E) the tertiary sector grew between 1950 and 2010 at the expense of primary and secondary jobs.

Answer: E

Feedback: The chart shows a steady decline, first in agricultural (primary sector) jobs as farmers left their farms and moved into factory work, and later in manufacturing (secondary sector) jobs as the economy became more based on services and factories shut down. The decline of farming continued during this time as well. The largest change was between 1950 and 2010 when the tertiary sector rose by 35 percent.

Chapter: 9: Economic Geography: Manufacturing and Services

Section: 9.5

AP Topic: 7.2 Economic Sectors and Patterns

9. A major difference between consumer services and producer services is that

(A) consumer services, unlike producer services, provide something that can be used up or consumed.

(B) producer services are performed for corporations, while consumer services are performed for individuals.

(C) the locational interdependence model does not apply to consumer services.

(D) the demand for consumer services far surpasses the demand for producer services.

(E) consumer services usually require workers to have a higher level of education than producer services do.

Answer: B

Feedback: Consumer services, such as entertainment, education, medical care, maid service, and the like, are performed for individuals. Producer services are performed for corporations and include things like financial and real estate services. There are other types of services as well, such as wholesale and retail sales, and government services. Locational interdependence is an issue for consumer services particularly since they need to be near their clients. A pizza shop must be near enough clients but not too near other competing pizza shops to stay in business. There is high demand for both consumer and producer services, particularly in developed countries. In developing countries, the number of services available may be limited. Many consumer services, such as janitorial work, do not require high levels of education, but most producer services do. Many companies have moved their call centers to India because many educated workers are available there.

Chapter: 9: Economic Geography: Manufacturing and Services

Section: 9.5

AP Topic: 7.7 Changes as a Result of the World Economy

10. According to the map of major cities in Figure 9.27 on page 313,

(A) New York, Rio de Janeiro, and Tokyo are the three most important cities for finance and world trade.

(B) consumer services are scattered in many cities around the world.

(C) highest-order producer services are concentrated in a few major cities.

(D) the many smaller cities that provide services negate the importance of the three largest cities.

(E) New York City is the only place with a major stock exchange and important financial services.

Answer: C

Feedback: The map shows New York, London, and Tokyo as the three highest-tier cities when it comes to major financial and world trade centers. All three have stock exchanges, and many financial services, international trading companies, etc. While B is a true statement, it is not shown on the map. Highest-order producer services are concentrated into a few major cities across the globe, which allows trade and financial operations to go on 24 hours a day.

Chapter: 9: Economic Geography: Manufacturing and Services

Section: 9.6

AP Topic: 7.6 Trade and the World Economy

Free Response Questions

1. Answer Parts A, B, and C below.

(A) Explain two major causes of the development of tourism.

(B) Give two examples and explain how the geography of a place affects tourism.

(C) Explain two consequences of tourism for developing countries.

(A) The rise of tourism has occurred as people in developed countries have become wealthier and have more free time to travel. Being able to leave one's job for any amount of time requires that a certain amount of money is made by the worker, and he/she also must be able to take time off from work, a benefit that is required in developed countries. In many developing countries, however, this is a luxury that most people do not have. Another cause for the rise of tourism is ease of transportation. It used to be difficult and expensive to travel very far, but with the advent of interstate highways and international airlines, travel has become much easier and safer.

(B) Tourism is affected by geography in many ways. Places exploit their geography to draw in tourists. Ski resorts are built in the Colorado Rockies and companies offer snorkeling vacations in the Bahamas. However, places are also constrained by their geography. The American Midwest is not someplace one can take a beach vacation, and people do not flock to Alaska to go swimming. Some places are extremely hard to get to, such as Nepal or Fiji, because of high mountains or remote island locations.

(C) A major consequence of tourism is that it can provide jobs and bring income to developing countries. Tourists have "discovered" the joys of visiting developing countries, seeing new cultures, and getting away from the bustle of life in the developed world. However, most tourism-related jobs are low income—maids, tour guides, etc.—and tourism can lead to exploitation of native populations. Sex tourism is extremely exploitative by its very nature.

Rubric: This question is worth six points, one for each of the causes in Part A, the examples/explanations in Part B, and the consequences in Part C.

Chapter: 9: Economic Geography: Manufacturing and Services

Section: 9.5

AP Topic: 7.8 Sustainable Development

2. Study the map in Figure 9.17 on page 304 to answer Parts A, B, and C below.

(A) Define the term *agglomeration* and explain how it pertains to high-tech industries in one of the following areas:

Silicon Valley, CA

Washington, D.C.

Research Triangle, NC

(B) Explain three important factors that lead to agglomeration in these areas.

(C) Explain one reason for commodity chains in high-tech industries.

(A) Agglomeration occurs when a certain type of industry becomes concentrated in a specific area along with other companies that supply the needs of the industry. Silicon Valley near San Francisco, CA, has many companies that are related to computer software such as Google, Facebook, Pixar, and others. As workers at these companies leave and form their own companies nearby, the agglomeration expands. Nearby universities provide students with the education they need to do this sort of work and often partner with companies for internships and research programs.

(B) Three important factors (aside from the proximity to universities mentioned above) that allow agglomeration are (1) availability of capital and people with entrepreneurial skills, (2) availability of good communication and transportation, and (3) a good "quality of life" for workers. This last one might not seem so important, but to attract and keep well-educated, qualified workers, it is a must.

(C) There are some parts of high-tech industrial work that do not need to be located near the agglomeration. Although the design of a product occurs in highly-educated, developed regions of the world, much of the actual manufacturing of high-tech products is done elsewhere. The iPhone may be designed in California, but it is assembled in China, where labor costs are much lower. Rare metals used in their construction come from Asia and Africa, and some components are made in Germany, Korea, Taiwan, and Japan. This type of commodity chain is frequent in the high-tech industries.

Rubric: This answer is worth seven points. The student gets a point for defining agglomeration, and a point for explaining the example of Silicon Valley. In Part B, each factor gets one point for a total of three, and the explanation of commodity chains in Part C gets two points.

Chapter: 9: Economic Geography: Manufacturing and Services

Section: 9.3

AP Topic: 7.2 Economic Sectors and Patterns

3. Answer Parts A, B, and C below.

(A) Explain one economic and one environmental reason that a business might outsource some of its work.

(B) Explain one consequence of outsourcing for developed countries and one consequence of outsourcing for developing countries.

(C) Explain one impact of governmental policies on outsourcing and provide a specific example.

(A) Outsourcing is when a company sends some of the work it needs to do away from the parent company to be done elsewhere. A company might outsource its call center to India or have its products assembled across the border in Mexico at a maquiladora plant. An economic reason to do this is to save money by paying foreign workers less than the company would have to pay their own workers at home. An environmental reason for outsourcing would be to avoid the stricter pollution laws found in developed countries by locating a factory in a place where laws are not as stringent.

(B) One consequence of outsourcing for a developed country is that jobs for less-skilled workers are transferred to other countries, causing unemployment and factory closures. The steel mills of Pennsylvania and car factories of Detroit are good examples of this. A consequence of outsourcing in developing countries is that new jobs become available and people move to be near the factories. A huge number of Mexican workers have migrated to near the border to work at the maquiladoras there.

(C) Governmental policies can help or hinder outsourcing. The NAFTA trade agreement between the United States, Mexico, and Canada has made trade easier between those countries and has fostered the growth of maquiladoras.

Rubric: This question is worth ten points. In Part A, it is important that the student give an economic and environmental reason for outsourcing. Each is worth two points. In Part B, each consequence and explanation is worth two points, and in Part C the example of NAFTA and its explanation are each worth a point.

Chapter: 9: Economic Geography: Manufacturing and Services

Section: 9.2

AP Topic: 7.7 Changes as a Result of the World Economy

CHAPTER 10
Economic Development and Change

AP Introduction

Chapter 10 introduces students to economic geography, specifically the topic of economic development. Chapter 10 focuses on the seventh content area of the College Board's AP Human Geography curriculum framework, Unit 7 Industrial and Economic Development, Patterns and Processes. Chapter 10 addresses the following AP Enduring Understandings from the AP Human Geography course framework:

- Economic and social development happens at different times and rates in different places.
- Environmental problems stemming from industrialization may be remedied through sustainable development strategies.
- Industrialization, past and present, has facilitated improvements in standards of living, but it has also contributed to geographically uneven development.

AP Concepts and Themes

Chapter Overview

This chapter contains fundamentals of the study of economic geography, including the following:
- Defining and measuring development is difficult due to the diversity of conditions and cultures across the world.
- Development levels and measures should be considered from the perspective of gender.
- Competing theories attempt to explain spatial differences in development.
- Economic development needs to be sustainable to avoid environmental degradation and loss of short-term gains.

Learning Objectives

- Explain causes and geographic consequences of recent economic changes, such as the increase in international trade, deindustrialization, and growing interdependence in the world economy.
- Explain the spatial patterns of industrial production and development.
- Describe social and economic measures of development.
- Explain how and to what extent changes in economic development have contributed to gender parity.
- Describe different theories of economic and social development.
- Explain how sustainability principles relate to and impact industrialization and spatial development.

Key Words

Use the terms below with a ▌ to focus your study of AP Human Geography key words in this chapter.

brain drain	gross domestic product (GDP)	▌semi-periphery
circular and cumulative causation	▌gross national income (GNI)	spread effect
▌core area	▌Human Development Index (HDI)	technology
core-periphery model	▌informal economy	technology gap
dependency theory	modernization theory	technology transfer
development	neocolonialism	Third World
▌ecotourism	neoliberal globalization	trickle-down effect
food security	▌periphery	underdevelopment
▌formal economy	purchasing power parity (PPP)	uneven spatial development
gender	remittances	▌World System Theory
▌Gender Inequality Index (GII)	▌Rostow's Stages of Economic Growth	

Note to the Teacher

The following Key Words appear in the AP Course Framework but are not called out as Key Words in the Bjelland Student Edition.

- *formal economy*: The aggregate production of goods and services that are regulated and known to government, as opposed to the informal economy.
- *Gender Inequality Index (GII)*: A measure of gender equality and progress developed by the United Nations Development Programme (UNDP) that emphasizes female reproductive health, educational attainment, and participation in political, management, professional, and technical positions.
- *Human Development Index (HDI)*: The most common tool for measuring human development is the Human Development Index (HDI). It is used by the United Nations (UN) to rank a country's level of human development. The three dimensions of development used to calculate a country's HDI are health, education, and living standards. The measure of health is determined by life expectancy at birth, or the average number of years a newborn infant can expect to live. Access to education is measured by examining mean, or average years of schooling and expected years of schooling. Living standards are measured by gross national income per capita, or the total value of goods and services produced by a country's economy each year measured per person.
- *Rostow's stages of economic development*: Economic historian Walt Rostow theorized that all developing economies pass through six stages of growth and advancement: (1) traditional societies, (2) preconditions for takeoff, (3) takeoff, (4) the drive to maturity, (5) the age of mass consumption, and (6) the postindustrial stage and rise of services.
- *world systems theory*: A theory developed by sociologist Immanuel Wallerstein arguing that international trade has led to a capitalist world economy. This world system is based on wealth and power and is arranged according to influence: the core (most dominant), the semi-periphery, and the periphery (least dominant).

▐AP▌ Chapter Discussion and Activities

Understanding Measures of Economic Development

AP ESSENTIAL KNOWLEDGE: Measures of social and economic development include Gross National Income (GNI) per capita; sectoral structure of an economy, both formal and informal; income distribution; fertility rates; infant mortality rates; access to health care; use of fossil fuels and renewable energy; and literacy rates.

TEACH: *Discuss the definitions of gross national product (GNP) and purchasing power parity (PPP) with students. Then explain that measuring economic development by means of a statistic like GNP requires refining the data by adjusting for PPP. This step is necessary as the cost of living differs, sometimes dramatically, from place to place.*

To help students appreciate this fact, ask them to investigate the cost of 5–10 basic household expenses in various U.S. states or metropolitan areas. Possible household expenses could include: monthly rent for a two-bedroom apartment; a gallon of regular (87 octane) gasoline; an average household's monthly electric bill; a pair of blue jeans, etc. Students should create a data table, making the individual household expenses the rows and the several states or metropolitan areas the columns. Each cell of the table will show the estimated cost of that item in that location. Then ask students to create a written analysis using their data table, reflecting on why a handful of simple household expenses cost different amounts in different places.

Investigating Labor Migration

AP ESSENTIAL KNOWLEDGE: Labor, transportation (including shipping containers), the break-of-bulk point, least cost theory, markets, and resources influence the location of manufacturing, such as core, semiperiphery, and periphery locations.

TEACH: *Tell students that the migration of skilled professionals from developing countries to developed countries is described as a brain drain. The United States benefits enormously from this on-going migration stream.*

Ask students to research the topic, using the following questions to guide their work: How many professionals in various occupations, such as doctors, nurses, engineers, lawyers, teachers, software designers, etc., come to the United States annually? From what countries do the largest numbers of professionals come?

Have students use their findings to create a map. Students can use a simple map of the world showing political boundaries and draw arrows from the source country to the United States. The width of the arrow should be proportional to the size of the migration stream. Maps should include labels for the name of the sending country and the estimated number of skilled professional immigrants. After students have completed their maps, ask them to write a brief report summarizing the patterns shown on their map and reflecting on the impact of the brain drain to the source country and the United States.

Identifying Sources of Economic Development

AP ESSENTIAL KNOWLEDGE: Different theories, such as Rostow's Stages of Economic Growth, Wallerstein's World System Theory, dependency theory, and commodity dependence, help explain spatial variations in development.

TEACH: *Remind students that many immigrants to the United States and other developed countries often send substantial amounts of money in aggregate to friends and family members in their home country. These remittances are an important source of income for developing countries. In some cases, one could consider them a source of foreign assistance.*

To help students appreciate the magnitude of this financial transfer, ask them to research the topic using reliable information sources. Some students could be assigned to look at the top ten destination countries for remittances leaving the United States, while other students might look at a single developing country and investigate the top five countries from which remittances are received.

After students have completed their research, ask them to share their findings with the class. Collect the data from all students to create a visual display of the information—a map, a table, a graph. Then use this to hold a class discussion on the patterns of the money flows and their significance in the economic development of the countries involved. To extend this activity, have a class discussion about other forms of foreign assistance that help stimulate economic development in developing countries.

Defining the Causes and Consequences of Economic Development

AP ESSENTIAL KNOWLEDGE: Complementarity and comparative advantage establish the basis for trade.

TEACH: *Tell students that each country in the world has its own path to economic development. Some countries are fortunate to have a substantial endowment of natural resources, such as petroleum or iron ore, which facilitated industrialization (e.g., Germany). Other countries created colonial empires and arranged the imperial economy to favor the country of origin (e.g., Great Britain). Favorable location near key trade routes made other countries rich through trade (e.g., Singapore).*

Give students a diverse group of five countries in various regions of the world and with differing levels of development. Ask them to research the geographic, historic, and economic circumstances behind each country's path to development. After considering the individual cases of the five countries, ask students to reflect on the countries as a group. What do the five examples suggest about the process of economic development?

Wrap up this activity by creating a short oral presentation with concise vignettes of the five countries. Students' presentations should include their "big-picture thoughts" about the process of development.

Investigating the Role of Women in Economic Development

AP ESSENTIAL KNOWLEDGE: The roles of women change as countries develop economically.

TEACH: *Discuss with students that, while the development of natural resources played a vital role in the past in creating economic development, increasingly the structure of the world economy favors places that possess well-educated workers. This human capital is seen as a key contributor in a dynamic economy. While most economically developed countries have expanded the rights of women over the past century, many less developed countries still limit women's roles in society through custom and law.*

Tell students to create a list of ways in which women in the United States sought greater freedoms over the past 100 years. These could be broadly considered to be legal, economic, medical, political, educational, or personal freedoms. Using this list, have students compare the situation in the United States today with 5–10 countries in different regions of the world, including Central or South America, Europe, Southwest Asia, South Asia, and Africa. Ask students to consider the following questions: Compared to the United States, do these individual countries show greater, equal, or lesser degrees of opportunity for women? For countries in which there are fewer opportunities for women, what is the overall level of economic and social development? How do these 5–10 countries compare to each other? Have students compile their findings in an annotated table.

Determining the Relationship Between Sustainability and Economic Development

AP ESSENTIAL KNOWLEDGE: Sustainable development policies attempt to remedy problems stemming from natural-resource depletion, mass consumption, the effects of pollution, and the impact of climate change.

TEACH: *Explain that for much of the past two centuries, pollution was a mere by-product of the era of industrialization. Businesses sought to maximize profits by avoiding the cost of dealing with pollutants created during production and not calculating the cost to society from consumption of potentially finite resources. More recently, an awareness of the need to limit pollution and adopt ways of running economies that are environmentally and economically sustainable have emerged.*

Have students form four small groups to discuss the underlying reasons for the emerging consciousness about sustainability. Ask each group to consider one of these four questions: (1) Why were businesses able to operate in an environmentally unsustainable manner for so long? (2) What has changed over the past half century such that increasing numbers of individuals, corporate leaders, government officials, and non-profit organizations are encouraging a new approach to economic development? (3) What constitutes sustainability in an environmental sense? In an economic sense? (4) Are environmental and economic sustainability compatible?

Once the groups have had time to discuss their questions and formulate answers, call on each group to share the response to their question with the class.

AP Chapter Feature Answer Key

Geography and Citizenship

1. Students' answers will vary. Students may need to conduct some outside research before completing their essays. Essays should reflect logical reasoning and include correct grammar, spelling, and punctuation.

2. Paragraphs will vary but should provide evidence to support students' positions.

3. Paragraphs will vary but should provide evidence to support students' positions.

4. Students may need to conduct some outside research as they prepare their oral presentations. Clear and concise arguments with supporting evidence should be included in students' presentations.

AP Test Practice Answer Key

Below are the Bjelland end-of-chapter AP Test Practice questions along with their answers, feedback, and rubrics.

Multiple Choice Questions

1. According to the Achievements of the Millennium Development Goals as listed in Table 10.1 on page 320,

(A) all regions have shown progress except sub-Saharan Africa.

(B) Southeastern Asia has made the least developmental progress.

(C) the education of female children has increased dramatically.

(D) all goals have been met other than the number of people living on $1.25 per day.

(E) all developing regions saw substantial progress, but there is still more to do.

Answer: E
Feedback: According to the table, all regions showed progress toward development in all aspects of their goals. None of them reached 0 percent for the first three or 100 percent for the last three, so there is still more to accomplish. Southeastern Asia has made the most progress. While it is true that the education of female children has increased dramatically, this is not one of the criteria measured in the table.
Chapter: 10: Economic Development and Change
Section: 10.3
AP Topic: 7.8 Sustainable Development

2. All of the following are aspects of the UN's Sustainable Development Goals EXCEPT

(A) ending poverty and hunger.

(B) promoting the rapid harvest from forest areas to provide raw materials for new factories in developing countries.

(C) reducing child and maternal mortality rates and eradicating diseases.

(D) increasing high school enrollment for girls and reducing discrimination against women.

(E) ensuring access to clean water, sanitation, and electricity.

Answer: B
Feedback: Answers A, C, D, and E are all found in the UN's goals. When it comes to using natural resources, the UN goals specifically highlight sustainability and conservation not rapid harvest by any means.
Chapter: 10: Economic Development and Change
Section: 10.3
AP Topic: 7.8 Sustainable Development

3. Lack of clean drinking water and sanitation in many urban slums leads to

(A) the spread of waterborne diarrheal diseases, such as cholera and dysentery.

(B) the need for governments to spend large amounts of money to bring water in by truck.

(C) the building of pipelines by charitable organizations and the United Nations.

(D) the lowering of maternal and infant mortality rates.

(E) successful rebellions among lower-class people who are angered by their treatment.

Answer: A
Feedback: Lack of sanitation and clean drinking water leads to the spread of disease, which increases maternal and infant mortality rates. Governments do not truck water in, although in some places, as development progresses, they are starting to build infrastructure to pipe in water and take away sewage.
Chapter: 10: Economic Development and Change
Section: 10.3
AP Topic: 7.8 Sustainable Development

4. According to the map in Figure 10.16 on page 332, access to the Internet

(A) is nearly 100 percent in developed countries.

(B) is less than 10 percent in some developing regions.

(C) is not available in some rural areas of highly developed countries.

(D) is not available to most people in sub-Saharan Africa and Australia.

(E) is available to a larger percentage of people in the United States than in Canada or Europe.

Answer: C

Feedback: Even though many developed countries have extremely high percentages of internet usage, there are still places in rural or remote areas where the Internet is not available. Europe, Canada, and Australia have the highest percentage of Internet availability, while sub-Saharan Africa and parts of the Middle East have the lowest.

Chapter: 10: Economic Development and Change

Section: 10.3

AP Topic: 7.3 Measures of Development

5. All of the following aspects of a country's physical geography affect its development EXCEPT

(A) the lack of availability of resources.

(B) overcrowding and overpopulation.

(C) whether or not the country is landlocked.

(D) poor soil productivity.

(E) a high instance of human, plant, and animal diseases in tropical climates.

Answer: B

Feedback: Jeremy Sachs, who has studied the relationship of physical geography to development, sees all the above as issues that affect development. Many countries lack resources and raw materials for industrial development. A landlocked country has difficulty trading with the outside world. Tropical climates tend to have poor soil productivity and many plant, animal, and human diseases. With overcrowding and overpopulation, however, the issue of physical geography is not the problem. The amount of available land for the number of people involved is the physical geography issue. Agricultural and physiological density are issues that lead to frequent famines, especially when paired with other issues like poor soil productivity.

Chapter: 10: Economic Development and Change

Section: 10.4

AP Topic: 7.5 Theories of Development

6. According to the idea of dependency theory,

(A) a dependent country is purposely kept in a state of lower development by the more-developed countries to further their own development.

(B) a country's development is dependent upon the amount of resources it has available, whether it is landlocked, and its climate.

(C) countries are dependent upon one another for trade and development aid in our global economy.

(D) countries in the periphery are dependent upon core countries to keep up their level of development.

(E) lower-class workers can unite to raise their standard of living.

Answer: A

Feedback: Dependency theory is an application of the Marxist theory that lower-class workers are exploited by factory owners. In this case, the factory owners are the more-developed countries, while the workers and raw materials are supplied by the developing nations. While Answer B is true that resources, location, and climate all affect development, this is not part of dependency theory. Answer C, about globalization, is also true but not part of dependency theory.

Chapter: 10: Economic Development and Change

Section: 10.4

AP Topic: 7.5 Theories of Development

7. The World Bank and IMF (International Monetary Fund) are important for development because

(A) they make loans to the governments of developing countries to aid in development.

(B) they provide funds to developed countries for modernization of aging infrastructure.

(C) they provide microloans to individuals so they can start up small businesses.

(D) they send advisors and administrators to take control of failing economies.

(E) they provide a place for people in developing countries to invest their money.

Answer: A

Feedback: The IMF loans money to developing countries to stabilize their economies or pay off debts, while the World Bank loans money to governments to use for infrastructure and other large development projects.

Chapter: 10: Economic Development and Change

Section: 10.5

AP Topic: 7.6 Trade and the World Economy

8. The UN Development Program does all of the following EXCEPT

(A) ranks countries according to their level of development.

(B) measures the poverty level of countries around the world.

(C) gives charity to groups in developing countries.

(D) ranks the development of men and women within countries separately.

(E) uses income, education levels, access to medical care, and other indicators to determine countries' standard of living.

Answer: C

Explanation: The UNDP uses its Human Development Index (HDI) to rank countries according to their level of development, which is computed by using income levels, access to medical care and education, and other statistics. The MPI and GDI compute levels of poverty and development based on gender, respectively. The UNDP provides money through various programs to aid in development, but it does not give charity.

Chapter: 10: Economic Development and Change

Section: 10.7

AP Topic: 7.3 Measures of Development

9. According to the Measuring Happiness table on page 344,

(A) a country's happiness directly correlates to the wealth of its citizens.

(B) citizens in developed countries are happier than people in developing countries.

(C) the happiest countries are all in Scandinavia and other cold climates.

(D) the least happy countries are all in sub-Saharan Africa.

(E) as standards of living rise, happiness increases.

Answer: D

Feedback: It would seem to make sense that as a country's standard of living rises, happiness would increase, but this is not always the case. The happiness of a country's citizens does not directly correlate to how wealthy the country is, whether the country is a developed country, or its climate. Cultural norms also affect happiness levels. However, countries with the lowest standard of living, true deprivation, tend to also have the lowest level of happiness, and they are all found in sub-Saharan Africa.

Chapter: 10: Economic Development and Change

Section: 10.7

AP Topic: 7.3 Measures of Development

10. Technology transfer is a goal of many development projects because

(A) it makes developing countries more dependent on core countries for their technology.

(B) it lessens the technology gap between developed and developing countries, allowing the latter to increase development.

(C) it aids large communication corporations to expand their networks worldwide.

(D) people in developing countries have little need for higher-level technology.

(E) due to lack of education, people in developing countries do not know how to use high level technology.

Answer: B

Feedback: There is a huge technology gap between developed and developing countries. A rise in technology and the knowledge of how to use it can help a country move from the periphery to the semi-periphery. People in developing countries need higher-level technology to interact with each other and with people in the more-developed world.

Chapter: 10: Economic Development and Change

Section: 10.3

AP Topic: 7.7 Changes as a Result of the World Economy

Free Response Questions

1. Answer Parts A, B, and C below.

(A)   Explain the impact of colonialism on the development of two countries.

(B)   Explain the impact of the slave trade on the development of the Americas and sub-Saharan Africa.

(C)   Explain the impact of colonization on one country in sub-Saharan Africa during the period of decolonization (1945–2000).

(A) Colonialism had different impacts on colonies, depending upon whether the native population of a country was replaced by colonists from the colonizing country. In colonies such as Canada and British North America, the native peoples were pushed out of their lands and replaced by French and British colonists, who eventually gained home rule. In places such as India and Gambia, where the Indian and Gambian people, respectively, were not replaced but merely ruled by Europeans to extract as much wealth and resources from the land as possible, self-rule did not happen so quickly. In North America, colonists were able to industrialize and trade, while in India and Gambia, European countries prohibited industrialization to keep resources flowing to the mother country and actively discouraged self-rule.

(B) The slave trade was part of the triangular trade between Europe, Africa, and the Americas. Manufactured goods, such as guns and rum, were sent to Africa where they were traded for enslaved people, who were in turn taken to the Americas and sold. The Americas then provided Europeans with sugar, cotton, and other raw materials. The slave trade aided in the development of the Americas, where enslaved people were used as agricultural laborers on plantations growing sugar cane, cotton, and other cash crops. The slave trade had an extremely detrimental effect in sub-Saharan Africa, however, where tribes fought one another to capture slaves for trade with Europeans, and able-bodied men and women were forced to leave their own lands to work in another.

(C) The decolonization of Africa in the late 20th century shows another problematic aspect of colonization. Since native populations had not been allowed to rule themselves, there was little practice of self-rule before decolonization. European nations often pitted one ethnic group against another to keep power, and when they left, borders were drawn without regard for which lands were claimed by various ethnic groups. The result was often civil war and sometimes genocide. Borders were often drawn instead for the convenience of the mother country to extract resources. A good example of this is Gambia, which is a long, narrow country whose borders track the river used to bring resources down to the ocean. The other three sides of the country are surrounded by Senegal, a border 330 miles in length.

Rubric: This question is worth ten points, two for the explanations of the impact of colonialism on each country in Part A, two for the effects of the slave trade on each country in Part B, and two points for the explanation and example of decolonization in Part C.

Chapter: 10: Economic Development and Change

Section: 10.4

AP Topic: 7.1 The Industrial Revolution

2. Answer Parts A, B, and C below.

(A)   Describe the path a country takes to development according to Rostow's stages of economic growth model. Explain one problem with using this model.

(B)   Explain Wallerstein's core-periphery model. Give an example of this theory at a global scale.

(C)   Give an example of core-periphery model at a national or local scale.

(A) According to Rostow's development model, a country goes through five stages to get to the highest stage of development. It begins with the traditional stage, in which people mainly practice subsistence farming and the country's productivity is low. Next, preconditions for takeoff are established when an external intrusion begins to cause political and economic change and entrepreneurs begin to invest in industries, transportation, and other infrastructure. In the takeoff stage, investment in industry grows and farming begins to become mechanized and more commercially oriented. In the drive to maturity stage, the country's economic output rises above its population growth, so people see their standard of living rise. They incorporate advanced technology into their businesses, which are more diversified and no longer only industrial. In the fifth stage, mass consumption, consumer goods and services rival industry. Finally in the postindustrial stage, industry starts to die out and is replaced by a more service-oriented economy. A problem with this model is that it only works at a national scale, and a second problem is that it assumes all countries will progress through these stages if they receive help from developed countries.

(B) Wallerstein's core periphery theory takes care of both problems. At the global scale, it divides up the world into the core countries (which are the main consumer countries, mainly service oriented, and the inventors of high tech products), the semi-periphery countries (which mainly produce the manufactured goods for the core countries), and the periphery countries (which provide the raw materials and labor). According to this model, a country can but might not move up to a higher level and it might even slip down to a lower one. A more pessimistic view (dependency theory) might even see the core countries purposely keeping lower-developed countries in that economic state for the good of the core countries. An example of this theory would be the relationship between the United States, Mexico, and other Central and South American countries, such as Guatemala and Colombia. Americans get a lot of tropical food products and other resources from Colombia, while Mexico provides a lot of manufactured goods in its maquiladora factories. All these goods go to the United States, which is the core consumer-based country.

(C) At a different scale, the core periphery theory works as well. New York City is a core area of the United States. The financial center in Manhattan, the stores of Fifth Avenue, and other businesses provide an array of services. Across the river in New Jersey is the semi-periphery area with many factories and oil refineries. Farther away is the periphery area, the countryside, which provides agricultural products and where many of the workers live who commute into the city.

Rubric: This question is worth eight points. Part A is worth three, one point for a cursory explanation of the Rostow model and two points if the model is well explained. A third point is awarded for the problem with the model. Part B is also worth three points, two for the explanation of the model, depending upon how well it is explained, and one point for the example given. Part C is worth two points, depending upon how well the example is explained.

Chapter: 10: Economic Development and Change
Section: 10.4
AP Topic: 7.5 Theories of Development

3. Answer Parts A, B, and C below.

(A) Explain the role of women in traditional agricultural economies. Give an example from either South America, Southeast Asia, or sub-Saharan Africa.

(B) Explain two ways that women's roles change as an economy becomes industrialized.

(C) Explain one way that developed countries can aid in helping women's economic prospects and one way that this may change their gender roles.

(A) In traditional agricultural economies, women work the fields with hoes and hand plows. They are also responsible for running produce stands at weekly markets to sell their goods. While men tend to own the land, women in subsistence economies tend to do the work on it. As horse-drawn plows and other more advanced technology are introduced, women tend to leave their agricultural roles. This gives them lower status in the family economy, leading to even more gender inequality. More than half the working women in sub-Saharan Africa and Southeast Asian countries, such as Nepal, are self-employed, working in the informal economy to sell their agricultural and hand-made products.

(B) As the economy becomes more industrialized, two things can happen. Men may leave the farms altogether to take factory jobs, which leaves women with all the agricultural work and the upkeep of the home and family. Unmarried women particularly may leave the village to work in factories as well, which changes their economic and cultural role completely. Now they are wage earners, and although they send a lot of their money home to family, they can spend money on themselves.

(C) Developed countries help developing countries in many ways. Transnational corporations often locate manufacturing plants in developing countries where the cost of land and labor is cheaper and pollution and labor laws are less stringent. This provides more jobs for both men and women. Groups, such as the Grameen Bank and Women for Women, make microloans to help people start small businesses. Many of these loans go to women. It changes their status in the household to have either a factory job or to own their own business. They are making a larger contribution to the family and, as such, may be afforded more power. This can run contrary to the subservient position required by cultural or religious beliefs in the country, and it can lead to women working to gain political rights for themselves.

Rubric: This question is worth nine points. In Part A, the answer receives two points for the explanation of the role of women in a traditional economy, one point for a simple answer and two points for a more fully developed one. A third point is gained for the example given. In Part B, the student can gain two points, one for each way that development changes the role of women. In Part C, the answer will gain a point for one way developed countries help developing countries and another point for the impact of that help on gender roles.

Chapter: 10: Economic Development and Change
Section: 10.6
AP Topic: 7.4 Women and Economic Development

CHAPTER 11

Urban Systems and Urban Structures

AP Introduction

Chapter 11 introduces students to urban geography with two main topics: the functions of urban places and the internal arrangement of cities. Chapter 11 focuses on the sixth content area of the College Board's AP Human Geography curriculum framework, Unit 6 Cities and Urban Land-Use Patterns and Processes. Chapter 11 addresses the following AP Enduring Understandings from the AP Human Geography course framework:

- The presence and growth of cities vary across geographical locations because of physical geography and resources.
- The attitudes and values of a population, as well as the balance of power within that population, are reflected in the built landscape.
- Urban areas face unique economic, political, cultural, and environmental challenges.

AP Concepts and Themes

Chapter Overview

This chapter contains fundamentals of the study of urban geography, including the following:
- Urbanization as a response to social change
- Contemporary developments in urban form
- Globalization's impacts on cities
- The size and distribution of cities
- Urban land use models
- Density and land use
- The role of infrastructure in urban places
- Urban design for sustainability
- Quantitative and qualitative data use
- Urban change
- Challenges to sustainable urban living and policy responses

Learning Objectives

- Explain the processes that initiate and drive urbanization and suburbanization.
- Explain how cities embody processes of globalization. Identify the different urban concepts such as hierarchy, interdependence, relative size, and spacing that are useful for explaining the distribution, size, and interaction of cities.
- Explain the internal structure of cities using various models and theories.
- Explain how low-, medium-, and high-density housing characteristics represent different patterns of residential land use.
- Explain how a city's infrastructure relates to local politics, society, and the environment.
- Identify the different urban design initiatives and practices.
- Explain the effects of different urban design initiatives and practices.

- Explain how the qualitative and quantitative data are used to show the causes and effects of geographic change within urban areas.
- Explain causes and effects of geographic change within urban areas.
- Describe the effectiveness of different attempts to address urban sustainability challenges.

Key Words

Use the terms below with a ▮ to focus your study of AP Human Geography key words in this chapter.

basic sector	▮ galactic city model	peripheral model
▮ bid-rent theory	gated community	▮ primate city
▮ blockbusting	▮ gentrification	▮ rank-size rule
▮ boomburb	▮ gravity model	▮ redlining
brownfields	▮ greenbelt	▮ sector model
▮ built landscape	hierarchy of central places	▮ site
central business district (CBD)	hinterland	▮ situation
central city	isotropic plain	▮ sprawl
central place	Latin American city model	▮ squatter settlement
▮ central place theory	▮ megacity	suburb
Christaller, Walter	▮ metacity	threshold
city	metropolitan area	town
▮ concentric zone model	▮ multiple nuclei model	urban geography
conurbation	multiplier effect	▮ urban hierarchy
▮ disamenity zone	network city	urban influence zone
economic base	▮ New Urbanism	urbanization
▮ edge city	nonbasic (service) sector	urbanized area
▮ exurb	peak land value intersection	▮ world city

Note to the Teacher

The following Key Words appear in the AP Course Framework but are not called out as Key Words in the Bjelland Student Edition.

- *megacity*: An urban area with more than 10 million inhabitants.
- *metacity*: An urban area with more than 20 million inhabitants.
- *sprawl*: The spreading of urban developments on undeveloped land near a city.
- *exurb*: A district outside a city, especially a prosperous area beyond the suburbs.
- *boomburb*: A large and rapidly growing suburb of more than 100,000 residents that is not the central city or largest city of a metropolitan area.
- *bid-rent theory*: A economic geography theory that refers to how the price and demand for real estate depends on the distance from the Central Business District (CBD).
- *built landscape:* The portion of the cultural landscape consisting of structures created by humans
- *greenbelt*: A land use planning technique to conserve open space whereby cities establish a perimeter beyond which new development is not permitted.
- *redlining*: A discriminatory real estate practice in North America in which members of minority groups are prevented from obtaining money to purchase homes or property in predominantly white neighborhoods. Redlining is officially illegal.
- *blockbusting*: A process in which real estate agents convince white property owners to sell their houses at low prices because of fear that black families will soon move into the neighborhood.
- *disamenity zone*: The very poorest part of a city that, in extreme cases, is not connected to regular city services.
- *squatter settlement*: A collection of buildings where the people have no legal rights to the land upon which they built. The people live there illegally and do not own the land.

AP Chapter Discussion and Activities

Understanding the Importance of Site and Situation to Urban Areas

AP ESSENTIAL KNOWLEDGE: Site and situation influence the origin, function, and growth of cities.

TEACH: *Ask students to investigate the influence of site and situation (absolute and relative location) on the establishment of urban places around the world. Students should pick their hometown, a city of importance in their home state, a city of importance in another U.S. state that they will likely know little about, and a city in a world region other than North America. For each city, students should determine what site influences (if any) led to the establishment of that urban place and how its present-day situation helps shape the city's existence.*

Have students share their findings by creating a large poster or an oral presentation using presentation software. Both posters and presentations should include maps and images to help convey the importance of site and situation to the cities they studied. To avoid considerable duplication of city choices, teachers can create short lists of diverse cities and assign a list to each student or to a group of students. After students have completed this activity, have a class discussion to identify any similarities and differences in patterns that students found during their research.

Using Data to Understand Changes in Urban Areas

AP ESSENTIAL KNOWLEDGE: Changes in transportation and communication, population growth, migration, economic development, and government policies influence urbanization.

TEACH: *To illustrate how data can be used to show the causes and effects of geographic changes within urban areas, ask students to research the top employers in their town, city, or a nearby community. Data on the number of employees can be often obtained from the business itself, the local chamber of commerce, or a municipal or county government. Data should be compiled in a table or spreadsheet.*

Have students use these questions to analyze the data they collected: For the largest 10–20 businesses in terms of the number of employees, which businesses are considered basic and non-basic? How many employees in total work for all of the basic sector businesses? What do the number of employees in the two types of business sectors indicate about the structure of the local economy? Considering this data, should local and/or state government act to change the ratio of basic to non-basic sector jobs in the community? Have students create a one- or two-page written analysis of the data.

Applying Central Place Theory

AP ESSENTIAL KNOWLEDGE: Principles that are useful for explaining urban concepts include rank-size rule, the primate city, the gravity model, and Christaller's central place theory.

TEACH: *Discuss with students that Walter Christaller developed his central place theory in an era when distance seemed to be a greater challenge than today. In the 1930s, individual car ownership would have been much more limited than today, meaning that getting to a store to purchase basic necessities was more of a challenge than today. People would be more likely in those days to minimize their travel by always seeking to patronize businesses in the closest possible central place at a given level in the urban hierarchy.*

Ask students to consider Christaller's ideas about the spatial arrangement of central places and consumer behavior considering the rise of e-commerce. All sorts of goods and services can be purchased over the Internet and delivered to the consumer, lessening the need for the customer to travel to obtain necessities. Students might comment upon the seemingly omnipresent trucks of commercial package delivery companies on the streets of their community or even the potential to have packages delivered by drone. Students will likely be able to draw insights from their own family's spatial behavior to comment on the topic. This activity could be carried out as class debate or by having students write a one-page essay on the issue.

Understanding Urban Land Use Models

AP ESSENTIAL KNOWLEDGE: Models and theories that are useful for explaining internal structures of cities include the Burgess concentric-zone model, the Hoyt sector model, the Harris and Ullman multiple-nuclei model, the galactic city model, bid-rent theory, and urban models drawn from Latin America, Southeast Asia, and Africa.

TEACH: *To help students understand the utility of the urban land-use models, review what a model is and how it can be used. Explain that models are an attempt at simplifying reality to focus on the essential characteristics. Detail is sacrificed to recognize the main issues. Models allow scholars to make general statements about the topic and then apply the models to new cases or examples. Does the model do a good job of explaining reality, or should it be refined considering a lack of explanatory power?*

With this background, ask students to study a city of more than 100,000 people in or near their home state. To avoid many students selecting the same city and to allow for comparison between cities in a region, you may wish to assign students to certain cities.

Students should create a simple sketch map of the city, labeling areas used for certain purposes like central business district, industry, residences, transportation, recreation, government facilities, etc. Key landmarks like prominent buildings, highways, or physical features should be included as well.

With their sketch maps complete, ask students to think about which of the urban land-use models (concentric circle, sector, multiple nuclei, or galactic) either singly or in combination seem to best represent the present-day land-use pattern of the study city. Students should present their answer in a brief written analysis to accompany their sketch map.

Explaining Gated Communities

AP ESSENTIAL KNOWLEDGE: Praise for urban design initiatives includes the reduction of sprawl, improved walkability and transportation, improved and diverse housing options, improved livability and promotion of sustainable options.

Criticisms include increased housing costs, possible de facto segregation, and the potential loss of historical or place character.

TEACH: *Tell students that gated communities have been a part of the cultural landscape in the United States for at least the last several decades. Ask students to investigate the reasons for this type of land use, going beyond the simple and obvious desire to prevent crime. Students should consider the following questions: Are there deeper, more fundamental reasons for this type of built environment? Likewise, with the popularity of gated communities, how do gated communities change the urban areas that surround them? Is the impact of gated communities positive, negative, or neutral, or does it depend upon one's vantage point? Organize students into small groups to exchange ideas on this topic, then ask the groups to share their findings with the entire class.*

Investigating Brownfield Sites

AP ESSENTIAL KNOWLEDGE: Responses to urban sustainability challenges can include regional planning efforts, remediation and redevelopment of brownfields, establishment of urban growth boundaries, and farmland protection policies.

TEACH: *Remind students that the United States is very much a post-industrial society, but the legacy of its industrial past is clearly visible on the landscape. Brownfield sites are property parcels with existing buildings in varying states of repair, derelict machinery or infrastructure, and possible environmental contamination. Brownfield sites often sit abandoned for decades due to the high costs of repurposing them compared to greenfield sites (undeveloped land).*

Ask students to select a brownfield site for study, using the following questions to guide their research: For what was the property used in the past? How long has it been abandoned or not fully utilized? How does the study site affect the community, both the immediate neighborhood as well as the entire town or city? Are there plans for redeveloping the property?

Students can acquire information about their study sites by visiting the neighborhood to directly observe the site, searching local media for articles and other coverage of the site, and speaking to people like government officials, environmental activists, company representatives, and neighbors of the site. Students should create a presentation that combines basic factual information about the brownfield site with their own analysis of the situation today. As students present their findings to the class, make time for questions and discussion of each brownfield site. What are the similarities and differences among them?

Connecting Globalization and Urbanization

AP ESSENTIAL KNOWLEDGE: Cities are connected globally by networks and linkages and mediate global processes.

TEACH: *Remind students that the process of globalization is multifaceted, but it essentially describes the increasing interconnections of places separated by considerable distance. Globalization is one influence upon urbanization, and globalization's impact on urban places can be seen in several ways.*

Ask students to form small groups to brainstorm the many ways in which the process of globalization is changing urban places. Students might consider a city of more than 100,000 inhabitants in or near their state as well as a city elsewhere in the world in which they have interest. Potential student responses could include businesses owned by foreign-based corporations, tourists, immigrants clustering in select neighborhoods, the presence of popular culture associated with other cultures/countries, among many possibilities. After firming up their own group's thoughts, each group should share their insights with the rest of the class.

AP Chapter Feature Answer Key

Geography and Citizenship

1. Students' papers should include specific examples of evidence to support their position on the issue. Papers should include correct grammar, spelling, and punctuation.

2. Students' tables should reflect an understanding the advantages and disadvantages of the "housing first" strategy.

3. Students' opinions on this issue will vary, but essays should include strong supporting evidence for the opinion expressed.

AP Test Practice Answer Key

Below are the Bjelland end-of-chapter AP Test Practice questions along with their answers, feedback, and rubrics.

Multiple Choice Questions

1. All of the following tend to increase urbanization EXCEPT

   (A) immigrants tend to settle in cities.

   (B) more jobs are available in cities as they industrialize.

   (C) people flee impoverished rural districts.

   (D) more services are available to people in cities.

   (E) there is more crime and pollution in cities.

   Answer: E
   Feedback: Urbanization began to grow quickly due to the availability of jobs during the Industrial Revolution, which provided work for impoverished rural areas. Immigrants also tended to settle in the cities where jobs and services are available. The fact that there is more crime and pollution in cities is a result of urbanization, not a cause of it.
   Chapter: 11: Urban Systems and Urban Structures
   Section: 11.1
   AP Topic: 6.1 The Origins and Influences of Urbanization

2. Global population, according to Figure 11.2 on page 350, has

   (A) become more rural as people become tired of the problems of city life.

   (B) become steadily more urban throughout the 20th century.

   (C) slackened in urban areas but grown quickly in rural areas since the 1950s.

(D) remained at about 50 percent urban and 50 percent rural through the second half of the 20th century.

(E) mainly concentrated in cities of more than a million people.

Answer: B
Feedback: Throughout the 20th century people have steadily moved from rural to urban areas all over the world.
Chapter: 11: Urban Systems and Urban Structures
Section: 11.1
AP Topic: 6.9 Urban Data

3. The world's largest urban areas, according to Table 11.1 on page 351,

(A) were almost all in Europe in 1900, but today all are found in periphery or semi-periphery countries.

(B) are found mainly in core countries today.

(C) have moved from predominantly U.S. cities to South American and African ones.

(D) have doubled in size since the 1950s.

(E) are found today on every continent in the world.

Answer: B
Feedback: From the time of the Industrial Revolution until the 1950s, almost all of the largest cities were in Europe or the United States. As populations slowed in developed countries and new countries industrialized, the cities with the highest populations were in China, India, and other developing nations.
Chapter: 11: Urban Systems and Urban Structures
Section: 11.1
AP Topic: 6.9 Urban Data

4. Christaller's central place theory is used to explain

(A) the spacing of interdependent urban settlements of different sizes in such a way that all the goods and services are provided to the people.

(B) the way that houses cluster around a central business district in cities.

(C) the importance of religious and political buildings within a city's central business district.

(D) the merging of separate cities into a megalopolis, like the Boston to Norfolk corridor.

(E) the movement of people to a city, causing urbanization to occur.

Answer: A
Feedback: Walter Christaller organized urban centers by size and mapped them in a series of interlocking hexagons. The larger the settlement, which provides more services, the larger the hexagon surrounding it. People in the rural area within each hexagon would go to that city for services. Outside the hexagon, they would go to another city of similar size.
Chapter: 11: Urban Systems and Urban Structures
Section: 11.5
AP Topic: 6.4: The Size and Distribution of Cities

5. If a country follows rank-size rule,

(A) there is one major city and many much smaller cities, which provide services to all the people equally.

(B) there is only one major city in the entire country, so many people go without services they need.

(C) there are two cities 1/2 the size of the largest city, ten cities 1/10 the size, and so on, allowing for services to be provided in all parts of the country.

(D) there are no big cities within the country, putting it very low on the development scale.

(E) the size of the government is much larger than necessary for the size of the country.

Answer: C
Feedback: Countries, such as the United States, Russia, and Canada, follow rank-size rule in which the second largest city is 1/2 the size of the largest, ten cities 1/10 the size, etc. There are usually two cities 1/2 the size, four cities 1/4 the size, etc. This allows services to be spread out over a large area of land so that everyone in the country can access the services they need.
Chapter: 11: Urban Systems and Urban Structures
Section: 11.5
AP Topic: 6.4: The Size and Distribution of Cities

6. In the central business district (CBD) of a city,

(A)   many people live in garden apartments and condos.

(B)   land costs are at their highest.

(C)   mass transit is often not available.

(D)   there are many big box stores, car showrooms, and multiplex movie houses.

(E)   urban slums and ghettoes are common.

Answer: B
Feedback: Few people live in the CBD. Those who do live in high rises because land is very expensive. Transportation into and out of the CBD is good. There are few large stores because of the cost of land; big box stores, movie houses, car dealerships, and cemeteries tend to be on the outskirts of town. Urban slums also tend to be outside of the CBD. Those in inner cities have often been rebuilt and gentrified.
Chapter: 11: Urban Systems and Urban Structures
Section: 11.6
AP Topic: 6.5: The Internal Structure of Cities

7. The peripheral model, also known as the galactic city model,

(A)   considers that cities are surrounded by rural land that supports the city by providing food and labor.

(B)   is a proposed model for cities in outer space.

(C)   is found mainly in Southeast Asia and sub-Saharan Africa.

(D)   is less accurate than the Hoyt Sector Model.

(E)   depicts the effects of beltway or ring road construction on a city and its inhabitants.

Answer: E
Feedback: When a beltway or ring road is built around a city, it changes the transportation patterns of the people. Much of their lives are spent in the suburbs and periphery of the city instead of in the city center. This model is called the peripheral or galactic city model, and it depicts more closely what cities are like today.
Chapter: 11: Urban Systems and Urban Structures
Section: 11.6
AP Topic: 6.5: The Internal Structure of Cities

8. All of the following are true about segregation within cities EXCEPT

(A)   segregation was forced upon African Americans by discriminatory housing practices such as redlining.

(B)   social and economic barriers make it difficult for members of some ethnic groups to move to wealthier areas of town.

(C)   some segregation is self-maintained, as seen in the persistence of areas known as Chinatown and Little Italy.

(D)   gated communities in many countries segregate the wealthier people of a city from the lower classes.

(E)   as the distance from the city center increases, the average age of the population also increases but the family size decreases.

Answer: E
Feedback: There are many ways that cities are segregated—by age, family size, wealth, ethnicity, and social groups. Many cities have a Little Italy, a Chinatown, or an area of the city known to be inhabited by members of a specific ethnic group. This is often self-maintained segregation since new immigrants will look for areas to live where people are like them and where language, religion, and aspects of culture are familiar. Other groups, such as African Americans, have had segregation forced upon them by redlining and other forms of discrimination. Many social and economic barriers can keep members of ethnic groups from moving out of their enclaves and into other areas of town. In many countries, gated communities keep members in and non-members out. As for age and family size, though, as the distance from the city increases, the age of the population decreases and the family size increases. Expensive, small apartments in the inner city are mostly the home of young urban professionals and older retired people who want the amenities without the travel. Married couples with children are more likely to live in suburbs where larger houses with yards are less expensive.
Chapter: 11: Urban Systems and Urban Structures
Section: 11.7
AP Topic: 6.10: Challenges of Urban Changes

9. The needs, problems, and patterns of women with respect to urban social space differ from men's in that

(A) there are more women than men, particularly as heads of households with children, and therefore the poverty rate is also higher.

(B) women travel farther to work than men and rely less on public transportation.

(C) jobs that are "women's work," such as clerical work, are concentrated in specific areas of the city.

(D) there are more opportunities for childcare in cities, which enables women to find better jobs.

(E) suburban women have more opportunities due to the variety of services available to them there.

Answer: A

Feedback: More women than men live in cities, and more women are poor, particularly women who are heads of household with children. In general, women travel less distance to work than do men, and jobs that are typically women's work are scattered throughout the city. Constraints on women in cities include lack of childcare and the need to work near available childcare. Suburban women have fewer opportunities due to the lack of services available nearby.

Chapter: 11: Urban Systems and Urban Structures

Section: 11.8

AP Topic: 6.7: Infrastructure

10. A major problem of urban growth in developing countries is

(A) high rise apartments that have been built to house the poor in inner cities.

(B) mixed-use areas of cities where rich and poor live near one another.

(C) central plazas that are being converted into business parks.

(D) informal squatter settlements that lack amenities.

(E) lack of schools and medical care for poor children.

Answer: D

Feedback: In developing countries, a major problem is that, as population growth has exploded, people have moved to cities in large numbers, and housing is not available for them. The poor make their own homes out of found materials. They are located on the outskirts of cities and lack basic services, such as running water, sanitation, and electricity. These squatter settlements or urban slums go by many names in different countries—favelas in Brazil, kampung in Indonesia—and are home to millions of people.

Chapter: 11: Urban Systems and Urban Structures

Section: 11.9

AP Topic: 6.10: Challenges of Urban Changes

Free Response Questions

1. Answer Parts A, B, and C below.

(A) Explain Christaller's central place theory.

(B) Define the term *primate city*, give an example, and explain the advantages or disadvantages.

(C) Define the term *rank-size rule*, give an example, and explain the advantages or disadvantages.

(A) Walter Christaller organized urban centers by size and mapped them in a series of interlocking hexagons. The larger the settlement, which provides more services, the larger the hexagon surrounding it. People in the rural area within each hexagon would go to that city for services. Outside the hexagon, they would go to another city of similar size.

(B) A primate city, such as London, Paris, or Mexico City, is much larger than the second largest city within its country. In small countries with good transportation systems, everyone can get to the primate city for services, but in developing countries or very large countries, people would not be able to get all the services they need.

(C) Countries, such as the United States, Russia, and Canada, follow rank-size rule in which the second largest city is 1/2 the size of the largest, the tenth largest city is 1/10 the size of the largest, etc. There are usually two cities 1/2 the size, four cities 1/4 the size, etc. This allows services to be spread out over a large area of land so that everyone in the country can access the services they need.

Rubric: This question is worth nine points. The student gains one point for explaining central place theory, a point for each definition of primate city and rank-size rule, a point each for examples of them, and two points each for the advantages and/or disadvantages.

Chapter: 11: Urban Systems and Urban Structures

Section: 11.5

AP Topic: 6.4: The Size and Distribution of Cities

2. Study the diagrams in Figure 11.24 on page 369. Then choose two of the urban models listed below, describe each one, and compare their advantages and disadvantages. Use a concrete example for at least one model.

(A) Burgess Concentric Zone Model

(B) Hoyt Sector Model

(C) Harris and Ullman Multiple Nuclei Model

(A) The Burgess Concentric Zone Model is the earliest city model of the three, describing a city in the 1920s. From the CBD, zones of housing radiate out in rings, starting with a zone of transition (warehouses and slums) and then a ring of small, inexpensive houses for workers. Next came a ring of wealthier homes on larger plots of land, and finally a commuter zone, which was just beginning to exist in the 1920s. The Burgess Model was meant to explain the growth and "look" of a city like Chicago in the early 20th century. This model shows how one type of housing merges into and then changes into another, as factory areas become zones of transition and small workers' homes deteriorate and become slums. One problem with this model is that it is old, so it does not consider the extensive road building and car culture that led to suburbs in the 1950s and 1960s. In today's cities, it is often true that the innermost ring of housing is the most expensive. Former factories are turned into loft apartments as areas that used to be slums are gentrified. It also does not consider the fact that many cities are on waterways or ports, which disrupt the concentric rings.

(B) The Hoyt Sector Model was proposed in the 1930s to explain why some areas (sectors) of cities are more highly valued, often due to their proximity to natural features like lakeshores or hills with beautiful views. Lower income housing occupies sectors that are near the heavy industry sectors and transportation corridors. This model considers that some areas of the city are more valuable than others and that new methods of public transportation had changed the look of cities in the 1930s. It still does not work for many of today's cities, however, since it does not take large suburban areas into account and there are no ring roads or beltways yet when this model was made.

(C) The Harris and Ullman Multiple Nuclei Model considers that many cities today have more than one center. There may be one central business district, but now that factory work is no longer the norm for most people, there may be other centers of work or entertainment that pull many workers and other people toward them. A city such as Baltimore, Maryland, has a large port, a tourist area called the Inner Harbor, a university district, and a hospital district. Each of these is surrounded by the types of services and workers' homes needed in that area. In addition, there are sectors of wealthier homes and lower-income housing interspersed within the city. This model still does not consider the advent of beltways and ring roads, which allow the spread of suburbs and of hubs of business at the intersection of beltways and major roads. The model that does this is called the galactic city or peripheral model.

Rubric: This essay is worth a total of ten points, two points for the explanation of each of the two required models, two points for the explanation of the advantages and disadvantages of the model, and two points for the required example. (Note: All three models are explained in this essay to make scoring easier, but only two of the three would be required for credit.)

Chapter: 11: Urban Systems and Urban Structures

Section: 11.6

AP Topic: 6.5: The Internal Structure of Cities

3. Answer Parts A, B, and C below.

(A) Identify and explain three problems associated with the inner city.

(B) Identify and explain one way that cities are dealing with one of the problems discussed in Part A.

(C) Identify and explain another way cities are dealing with another of the problems discussed in Part A.

(A) One problem associated with the inner city is traffic jams. As people come into the city each day for work and leave each evening to go back to their suburban homes, roads become clogged with traffic. Choke points such as bridges or places where major roads meet are often the site of accidents that can jam the roads for hours. Cities try to deal with this problem by increasing spending on public transportation, such as building subway lines and providing buses. Cities also try to encourage people to carpool or bike to work by building special HOV lanes and bike lanes.

(B) Another problem associated with the inner city is gentrification. Developers buy up slum housing and either fix it up or tear it down and build high-priced apartments. They then rent or sell them at a much higher price, often to young urban professionals. The original tenants of the low-cost housing, who are often minorities, cannot afford the newly built rentals and must find other places to live. Gentrification changes the entire culture of neighborhoods, driving out small ethnic restaurants and mom-and-pop stores in favor of trendy coffee shops and high-priced restaurants. The answer to this is for city governments to make laws requiring the building of mixed-use housing, where some of the units are designated for low-income residents.

(C) A third problem associated with inner cities is decaying infrastructure. Often the central parts of cities are the oldest, original parts of the city, and so their bridges, buildings, sewer and water lines, and electricity grids, etc., are also very old. Many cities originally had factories, which have since gone out of business and been abandoned. City governments can do something about this by launching urban renewal initiatives, offering tax breaks and other incentives to builders who will turn brownfields and abandoned buildings into loft apartments, mixed-use shopping areas, arts districts, and more. This can, unfortunately, lead to gentrification, but it can also turn high crime, blighted areas of the city into beautiful and economically viable urban centers.

Rubric: The answer is worth ten points, two for each explanation of the three urban problems, and two for each possible fix for the problem. (Note: A fix was provided for all three urban problems here, but only two are required.)

Chapter: 11: Urban Systems and Urban Structures

Sections: 11.7 and 11.8

AP Topic: 6.11: Challenges of Urban Sustainability

CHAPTER **12**

The Political Ordering of Space

AP Introduction

Chapter 12 introduces students to political geography with an emphasis on sovereign states. Chapter 12 focuses on the fourth content area of the College Board's AP Human Geography curriculum framework, Unit 4 Political Patterns and Processes. Chapter 12 addresses the following AP Enduring Understandings from the AP Human Geography course framework:

- The political organization of space results from historical and current processes, events, and ideas.
- Political boundaries and divisions of governance, between states and within them, reflect balances of power that have been negotiated or imposed.
- Political, economic, cultural, or technological changes can challenge state sovereignty.

AP Concepts and Themes

Chapter Overview

This chapter contains fundamentals of the study of political geography, including the following:
- Basic terminology in political geography
- The global state system
- The spatiality of political power
- Types of political boundaries
- The functions of political boundaries
- Electoral geography
- Unitary and federal systems of administration
- Defining devolutionary factors
- The erosion of sovereignty
- Centripetal versus centrifugal forces

Learning Objectives

- For world political maps: (a) define the different types of political entities; (b) identify a contemporary example of political entities.
- Explain the processes that have shaped contemporary political geography.
- Describe the concepts of political power and territoriality as used by geographers.
- Define types of political boundaries used by geographers.
- Explain the nature and function of international and internal boundaries.
- Define federal and unitary states.
- Explain how federal and unitary states affect spatial organization.
- Define factors that lead to the devolution of states.
- Explain how political, economic, cultural, and technological changes challenge state sovereignty.
- Explain how the concepts of centrifugal and centripetal forces apply at the state scale.

Key Words

Use the terms below with a ▮ to focus your study of AP Human Geography key words in this chapter.

▮ antecedent boundary

artificial boundary

autonomous nationalism

▮ autonomous region

▮ centrifugal force

▮ centripetal force

▮ choke point

▮ colonialism

compact state

▮ consequent (ethnographic) boundary

core area

▮ devolution

electoral geography

elongated state

enclave

▮ ethnic cleansing

▮ ethnic separatism

European Union (EU)

exclave

exclusive economic zone (EEZ)

▮ federal state

fragmented state

▮ functional dispute

▮ geometric boundary

geopolitics

▮ gerrymandering

▮ imperialism

▮ irredentism

landlocked

▮ multinational state

▮ multistate nation

▮ nation

nationalism

▮ nation-state

natural boundary

▮ neocolonialism

perforated state

physical boundary

political geography

positional dispute

prorupt state

reapportionment

redistricting

regionalism

▮ relic boundary

resource dispute

▮ self-determination

separatism

▮ shatterbelt

▮ state

▮ stateless nation

subnationalism

▮ subsequent boundary

▮ superimposed boundary

▮ supranationalism

territorial dispute

▮ territoriality

▮ terrorism

▮ unitary state

United Nations Convention on the Law of the Sea (UNCLOS)

Note to the Teacher

The following Key Words appear in the AP Course Framework but are not called out as Key Words in the Bjelland Student Edition.

- *stateless nation*: A group that identifies itself as a nation based on common ethnic, linguistic, and religious identity but that lacks majority status in any nation-state.
- *multinational state*: A state that contains two or more ethnic groups that agree to coexist peacefully by recognizing each other as distinct nationalities.
- *multistate nation*: A nation that stretches across borders and across states.
- *autonomous region*: An area of a country that has a degree of autonomy or has freedom from an external authority.
- *sovereignty*: The right of self-governance as a state, whereby other states acknowledge that status.
- *self-determination*: The right of a group to govern itself in its own state or territory.
- *colonialism*: The practice of a country acquiring political control over another country or territory, occupying it with settlers, and exploiting it economically.
- *imperialism*: The forceful expansion by a state with the objective of taking permanent and pervasive control over large areas of land, with the goal of spreading the state's culture, economic system, and form of governance to the conquered lands.
- *shatterbelt*: A term from geopolitics indicating a region of countries or territories with internal conflicts that could become the location of conflict between the major powers.
- *choke point*: A term from geopolitics indicating a narrow body of water like a strait or canal where the application of force by a state could halt the commercial shipping activity of a rival state.

Defining Political Geography

AP ESSENTIAL KNOWLEDGE: Types of political entities include nations, nation-states, stateless nations, multinational states, multistate nations, and autonomous and semiautonomous regions, such as American Indian reservations.

TEACH: *One way to characterize the field of political geography is to say it is the geography of power. Ask students to consider the various types of power in society—administrative, legal, military, economic, moral, cultural, sexual, and possibly others. Ask students to consider how each of these have a spatial (locational) expression. More narrowly, how do governments control or structure space? Organize students into small groups to discuss these questions. Then have the groups share their findings with the entire class.*

Identifying Unitary and Federal States

AP ESSENTIAL KNOWLEDGE: Unitary states tend to have a more top-down, centralized form of governance, while federal states have more local-based, dispersed power centers.

TEACH: *Explain that while most of the world's states use a unitary system of government, the federal system is still a very important alternative. Ask students to investigate the usage of federal systems around the world, using the following questions to guide their research: Which countries other than the United States use a federal system? What do the various federally-organized countries have in common? Why might they have chosen to use a federal system? A variant of the federal system is the confederal structure. Why are there so few countries that use a confederal system?*

Have students organize their findings by creating a poster that includes columns for the country name, federal/confederal choice, and assorted details about that country's geography that pertain to its choice of government system.

Categorizing Types of Political Boundaries

AP ESSENTIAL KNOWLEDGE: Types of political boundaries include relic, superimposed, subsequent, antecedent, geometric, and consequent boundaries.

TEACH: *Help students understand the various types of political boundaries by studying a local example. This could be a town/city, county or your state. Which of the boundary types are represented by the political unit they selected? Why do the students think the political unit's boundaries were placed in those locations? To avoid considerable duplication in the political units chosen by the students, you can create a list of area political units from which the students can be assigned a topic or can request a topic.*

Comparing and Contrasting Centrifugal and Centripetal Forces

AP ESSENTIAL KNOWLEDGE: Centrifugal forces may lead to failed states, uneven development, stateless nations, and ethnic nationalist movements.

Centripetal forces can lead to ethnonationalism, more equitable infrastructure development, and increased cultural cohesion.

TEACH: *Discuss with students that the balance between the strength of centripetal (unifying) and centrifugal (disunifying) forces helps explain the circumstances of countries. Ask students to investigate three countries of their choice, one for each of the following categories: (1) a country that lost a significant portion of its territory through secession or was completely dissolved since 1900; (2) a country that faces a serious threat of secession or disintegration today; and (3) a country that has no serious threat of secession or disintegration today. To avoid substantial duplication of countries, the teacher may wish to coordinate which countries are chosen.*

For each of the three types of countries, students should research the centripetal and centrifugal forces, sharing their findings for each country in a written report. Then ask students to reflect on the experiences of all three countries, by considering these questions: What do the three examples indicate about national unity, ethnicity, nationalism, and administrative system? Discuss students' responses as a class.

Understanding the Process of Gerrymandering

AP ESSENTIAL KNOWLEDGE: Voting districts, redistricting, and gerrymandering affect election results at various scales.

TEACH: *Remind students that in the United States, gerrymandering has attracted considerable attention over the past few years from journalists, politicians, scholars, and voters. While gerrymandering for racially discriminatory purposes is unconstitutional, gerrymandering for partisan advantage is generally permitted. Ask students to research the situation in their state, using the following questions to guide their research: Is gerrymandering permitted in their state according to the state constitution, state law, or judicial ruling? Are there prominent examples of gerrymandering, perhaps with U.S. House of Representatives districts, or districts in the state legislature? How is redistricting accomplished in that state, by the state legislature, a special commission appointed by the state legislature, or by a non-partisan organization? Have students share their findings in a brief report, which should include any maps of gerrymandered districts they discover from the research.*

Investigating Cases of Territoriality

AP ESSENTIAL KNOWLEDGE: Territoriality is the connection of people, their culture, and their economic systems to the land.

TEACH: *Explain that territoriality is the human attachment to place and the desire to control and defend that place from encroachment or threat by others. How humans seek to defend a place or area they consider their own takes many forms, depending on the society, the political system in which the people live, the nature of the challenge to territoriality, and the scale (local, regional, national, international) of the challenge.*

Ask students to select a conflict anywhere in the world and consider it using these questions: (1) What is the place/area under dispute? (2) Who are the people expressing a territorial claim to that place? (3) What forms of power (military, political, legal, economic, demographic, cultural, moral, etc.) are used by the contesting parties to organize space in their favor? (4) What is the status of the selected conflict? Have students present their findings in an oral presentation or a written report. Presentations and written reports should include maps of the area of conflict.

Connecting History and Political Geography

AP ESSENTIAL KNOWLEDGE: Colonialism, imperialism, independence movements, and devolution along national lines have influenced contemporary political boundaries.

TEACH: *Discuss with students how political geographic analysis often draws upon the study of history to understand how past distributions of power contributed to the present-day arrangements. An important example of this relationship is the state system and sovereign boundaries, many of which are the by-product of colonial administration.*

Ask students to investigate the lingering impact of colonial boundaries both between sovereign states and within a sovereign state. Each student should select two boundaries, one international and one internal, to study. Students should consider the following questions in their study: (1) What actor (country, ruler, company, explorer, etc.) determined the location of the boundary? (2) Why was the boundary placed in that location? In other words, what advantage was sought by organizing space this way? (3) When was the boundary established? (4) How has the boundary functioned over time, including at the present?

The United States and Canada are both good choices for this activity. Since so much of the world was under colonial rule from the 17th through the 20th centuries, there are many possibilities for boundary choices. Have students present their findings in an oral presentation or a written report. Presentations and written reports should include maps of the area of study.

AP Chapter Feature Answer Key

Geography and Citizenship

1. Students' paragraphs should reflect an understanding of the issue and include evidence to support their positions.

2. Encourage students to do some outside reading on this issue before writing their position papers. Perhaps there are specific, real-world examples that could help students decide their position on the issue. Students' papers should address each of the questions presented and include evidence to support their position.

3. Student pairs should work together to understand both sides of the issue. Some outside research may be necessary as students prepare for the debate. Students should follow common debate process and provide clear, factual information to support their argument.

4. Students' essays should present clear reasoning and evidence. Essays should include correct grammar, spelling, and punctuation.

5. Students' answers will vary but should reflect an understanding of the advantages and disadvantages of using independent commissions as an approach to electoral redistricting.

AP Test Practice Answer Key

Below are the Bjelland end-of-chapter AP Test Practice questions along with their answers, feedback, and rubrics.

Multiple Choice Questions

1. The term *stateless nation* is used to signify

(A) an area of land that is uninhabited.

(B) an area of land that is being fought over by two neighboring states.

(C) a group of people possessing a common culture but no land.

(D) a group of people who have fled to another country to escape violence in their own country.

(E) a territory claimed by several other countries.

Answer: C

Feedback: The term *nation* is used to signify a group of people who have a common culture. If they do not control the territory that was traditionally theirs, they are called a stateless nation. The Kurds or Basques are good examples.

Chapter: 12: The Political Ordering of Space

Section: 12.1

AP Topic: 4.10 Consequences of Centrifugal and Centripetal Forces

2. The fact that European states ignored ethnic groups' cultural boundaries when creating political boundaries in Africa led to

(A) the return of several African states to territorial status.

(B) the rise of peaceful multiethnic states in much of sub-Saharan Africa.

(C) the continuation of European dominance in sub-Saharan Africa.

(D) significant ethnic diversity and many conflicts over borders.

(E) the loss of many ethnic groups' cultural heritage.

Answer: D

Feedback: When decolonization of Africa occurred after World War II, European states drew boundaries and formed new sovereign states out of the multitude of ethnic groups in their former African colonies. They disregarded territorial claims by various ethnicities and split some ethnic groups between countries. The result was ethnic strife and war, both international and civil, as ethnic groups sought to reunite or to take back territory.

Chapter: 12: The Political Ordering of Space

Section: 12.1

AP Topic: 4.8 Defining Devolutionary Powers

3. Challenges to the sovereign power of the state include all of the following EXCEPT

(A) globalization of economies and the proliferation of transnational organizations whose economic decisions are not limited to the importance of one state.

(B) the rise of international organizations whose agreements limit the power of the state.

(C) the emergence and growth of non-governmental organizations that unite members around a common cause rather than a state.

(D) massive international migration flows and separatist movements that undermine the cultural unity of the state.

(E) the rise of right-wing nationalist political movements that aim to curb immigration and limit the power of international and transnational organizations.

Answer: E

Feedback: The definition of a state is an area of territory which has sovereign power. In other words, it runs itself and no other entity has control over it. Many things challenge the sovereignty of states today, including the interests many companies have in more than one state, groups such as the UN can make agreements that are binding to states, NGOs work in many states simultaneously, and migration and separatist movements undermine cultural unity. However, within many states, right-wing separatist movements have sought to counter the challenges by curbing immigration and seeking to put their own state's agenda ahead of the global one.

Chapter: 12: The Political Ordering of Space

Section: 12.1

AP Topic: 4.9 Challenges to Sovereignty

4. The disadvantages of an extremely large country, like Russia, China, or Canada, include all of the following EXCEPT

(A) much of the land may be remote and therefore underdeveloped.

(B) it may not encompass enough viable agricultural land to feed its people.

(C) it is hard to govern and control such a large area.

(D) it is more likely to have a culturally homogenous population.

(E) large size is not a guarantee of mineral resources, which are often difficult to use if they are found in remote areas.

Answer: D

Feedback: We think of large countries as naturally being powerful and strong, but they usually contain a core area where most of the population lives, the food is grown, and the industries flourish, while the rest of the territory is sparsely populated, lacks services, and is largely unregulated. A culturally homogenous population is not usually found in large countries because various ethnic groups may live in different regions. Canada, for example, has the French-speaking Quebecois on the eastern coast, English-speakers in the middle and west of the country, and various Native American tribes in the north.

Chapter: 12: The Political Ordering of Space

Section: 12.1

AP Topic: 4.3 Political Power and Territoriality

5. Lesotho, San Marino, and Vatican City are all categorized as

(A) exclaves.

(B) nation states.

(C) multiethnic states.

(D) enclaves.

(E) perforated states.

Answer: D

Feedback: The definition of an enclave is a sovereign state or a part of a sovereign state that is totally enclosed by another state. Lesotho is surrounded by South Africa, while San Marino and Vatican City are surrounded by Italy. The state that is surrounding them is called a perforated state.

Chapter: 12: The Political Ordering of Space

Section: 12.1

AP Topic: 4.1 Introduction to Political Geography

6. The proliferation of tiny island countries that are recognized as sovereign states causes

(A) issues to arise about the Law of the Sea and its 200-nautical-mile limits.

(B) arguments about their representation in the United Nations.

(C) attacks on larger states by small states that need their resources.

(D) transnational companies to form to facilitate trade.

(E) the rise of dictatorships and other non-democratic governments.

Answer: A

Feedback: Since decolonization after World War II, many tiny islands have become separate countries. They are sometimes important because of mineral wealth or as a stopping-off place for ships. Representation in the United Nations, while a problem, does not pertain only to small island states. Attacks by larger countries to gain resources or ports do occur, but smaller states would not usually attack larger ones. The main issue with small island states is that they can claim a 200-nautical mile limit around their island, which sometimes conflicts with that of other islands or with countries on the mainland.

Chapter: 12: The Political Ordering of Space

Sections: 12.1 and 12.2

AP Topic: 4.6 The Function of Political Boundaries

7. A government in which the entire country is under the jurisdiction of a national government located in the capital city without smaller regional governments is called

(A) a stateless nation.

(B) a compact state.

(C) a unitary system.

(D) a federal system.

(E) a confederation.

Answer: C

Feedback: A federal system of government has separate states which have been granted certain sovereign powers by the constitution. In a unitary system the only sovereign entity is the national government, located in the capital city, and all law emanates from there. In a confederation, the national government has very little power and the states are supreme. The term *stateless nation* has to do with a group of people, not a country, because they do not have one. A compact state refers to the shape of a state, not its government.

Chapter: 12: The Political Ordering of Space

Section: 12.1

AP Topic: 4.7 Forms of Governance

8. To trade successfully, a landlocked country like Bolivia must

(A) make treaties with neighboring states that allow trade through their territory.

(B) make war against neighboring states to gain sea access.

(C) build airports to bring goods in and out of the country.

(D) build canals that bring water trade into the country.

(E) appeal to the United Nations to force other countries to let them trade.

Answer: A

Feedback: Bolivia, although landlocked, has the distinction of being able to trade through ports on two oceans because of the treaties they have made with Argentina on one side and Chile and Peru on the other. Although making war is another way to gain access to trade, it is rarely successful and is very costly. Trade by air is also extremely expensive and building canals does not work without the consent of the country through which the canal will pass. Appeals to the UN might be attempted but that organization cannot force another country to allow trade to pass through its lands.

Chapter: 12: The Political Ordering of Space

Section: 12.1

AP Topic: 4.5 The Function of Political Boundaries

9. Terrorism is a geographic issue because

(A) it can be domestic or international in scale, and specific countries harbor or assist terrorists.

(B) it causes fear all over the world when a terrorist attack occurs.

(C) it is specifically found only in certain parts of the world.

(D) terrorists are usually from developing countries while their targets are developed countries.

(E) increased security measures cause a lack of cooperation between countries.

Answer: A

Feedback: Terrorism does cause fear all over the world, but the most important and geographic questions regarding terrorism are 1) are the terrorists foreign or domestic? and 2) are they being helped by other countries? Terrorism is found all over the world and has brought about increased cooperation between countries trying to foil terrorist plots or bring terrorists to justice. It is untrue that terrorists are usually from developing countries or that they only target wealthier states. Timothy McVeigh, who perpetrated the Oklahoma City bombing, was from the United States, and Basque and Irish terrorists, who are from Spain and Ireland respectively, wreaked havoc for years in Europe.

Chapter: 12: The Political Ordering of Space

Section: 12.1

AP Topic: 4.8 Defining Devolutionary Factors

10. Gerrymandering, the convoluted drawing of political districts to disenfranchise a group of people,

(A) happens mainly in unitary systems of government, not in federal or confederal systems.

(B) is never a problem in the United States because of congressional oversight of the process.

(C) was a problem in the early 20th century when white politicians used it to take away voting power from African Americans, but it no longer occurs in the United States.

(D) is a problem today when the political party in power in a state is able to take votes away from other political parties.

(E) is mainly a problem in developing countries where politicians are corrupt and susceptible to bribery.

Answer: D

Feedback: Gerrymandering is a problem in federal systems of government that apportion delegates by population like the United States. This type of government must reapportion the delegates, like the United States does every ten years, to account for population growth, and in-migration and out-migration. Gerrymandering was originally used in the United States to disenfranchise African Americans. Now the problem tends to be more based on political party. In an overwhelmingly Republican state like Texas, the districts have been redrawn by that party to make sure that Democrats get very few representatives. In a majority Democratic state like Maryland, the Democratic Party has insured that there are very few majority Republican districts.

Chapter: 12: The Political Ordering of Space

Section: 12.3

AP Topic: 4.6 Internal Boundaries

Free Response Questions

1. Answer Parts A, B, and C below.

(A) Define the terms *natural* or *physical boundary, geometric boundary,* and *superimposed boundary,* giving an example of each.

(B) Explain how one of the types of boundaries can lead to border disputes.

(C) Explain how a second type of boundary can lead to border disputes.

(A) A natural or physical border between states is part of the physical geography of the landscape, like an ocean, a river or the crest of a mountain range. The Atlantic Ocean and the Rio Grande are examples of natural borders of the United States. A geometric border is one that is drawn using latitude and longitude lines, such as the one between the western United States and Canada. A superimposed border is one that is made by the colonizing country on its former colonial holdings, often without regard to issues of ethnicity and tribal territory, such as occurred in Rwanda in sub-Saharan Africa during decolonization.

(B) A natural border or boundary would seem to be set in stone, but mountain ridges can erode or fall due to earthquakes. Countries argue about whether to count the top of the mountain or the watershed divide as the border, as in the case of China and India. Rivers are problematic because they can change course and are often very fertile, valuable land where many people live. The Rhine River between Germany and France is a good example, and it caused border disputes over hundreds of years.

(C) A superimposed boundary often causes border disputes because it does not consider the ethnic makeup of a country or the territorial claims of various ethnic groups. As mentioned above, the creation of the country of Rwanda, which included the ethnic groups known as Hutus and Tutsis, led to civil war and attempted genocide as the two groups fought for territorial control.

Rubric: This answer is worth seven points. Each definition and example is worth one point in Part A. (Note that the student must get the definition AND example correct in order to get one point.) In Parts B and C, each explanation is worth two points. To get the second point, there must be a specific, well-explained example.
Chapter: 12: The Political Ordering of Space
Section: 12.1
AP Topic: 4.4 Defining Political Boundaries

2. Answer Parts A and B below.

    (A) Define the terms *centrifugal force* and *centripetal force*.

    (B) Describe how these forces affected a country in three of the following regions: Europe, Southeast Asia, sub-Saharan Africa, the Middle East.

(A) A centrifugal force is one that can pull a country apart, causing disunity among its people, while a centripetal force is a unifying force which brings a country closer together.

(B) A good transportation and communication system within a country is a unifying or centripetal force. It facilitates trade and political integration. Government control of roads and communication with the outside world fosters unity within a country, as well, by keeping out foreign elements of culture and curtailing immigration. Nationalism can be both a centripetal force, unifying a group of people with the same culture, language, nationality, etc., into one strong country and a centrifugal force, tearing apart an empire made up of different ethnic groups. Jewish nationalism, for example, aided in the formation of the state of Israel, since Jews from all over the world longed to be united into one country. On the other hand, nationalism caused the breakup of Yugoslavia into the separate ethnically different countries of Serbia, Croatia, Bosnia, and others. Another centripetal force is strong institutions, such as religion and schools. Schools teach the country's history and values to children, while religion does much the same. If most of the people within a country are of the same religion, such as being Buddhist in Thailand or Hindu in Nepal, it is a unifying factor. If there are two or more powerful religious groups, such as Shi'ite and Sunni Muslims in the Middle East, religion can also be a centrifugal force.

Rubric: This answer is worth seven points. The student gets one point for defining centrifugal and centripetal forces. (Note that both terms need to be defined correctly to receive credit.) The other six points are awarded for discussion of centrifugal and centripetal forces in each of three regions. In the above example, the student discussed specific forces, giving examples from Israel and the Middle East in general, Yugoslavia in Europe, and Thailand and Nepal in Southeast Asia.
Chapter: 12: The Political Ordering of Space
Section: 12.1
AP Topic: 4.10 Consequences of Centrifugal and Centripetal Forces

3. Answer Parts A, B, and C below.

    (A) Define and explain the importance of transnational organizations in politics and the economy.

    (B) Define and give two examples of supranational groups at the global scale.

    (C) Identify and explain the importance of supranational organizations at the regional scale, using two examples of political, economic, or social effects.

(A) The term *transnational* is usually applied to large businesses which are multinational corporations. In other words, while they may be headquartered in one country, they have offices, factories, and outsourced call centers in many countries. They cannot, however, make laws or regulations for the countries in which they are located. Transnational corporations facilitate the movement of money and goods around the world, provide many jobs in developing countries, and play a vital part in the global economy. Transnational groups can influence politics in the countries where they locate because they play an extremely important role in the economy, particularly in developing countries. A country like Bangladesh, which wants to attract and keep textile factories to provide jobs for its people, may make laws discouraging the formation of unions, for example.

(B) Supranational organizations are made up of representatives from various countries and can make agreements and laws that are binding upon member countries. The United Nations, for example, is a global supranational organization, made up of representatives from almost every country in the world, that can send its peacekeeping forces into countries that are having civil wars or can vote to place sanctions on countries that are not following the wishes of its members. Affiliates of the United Nations, such as the World Health Organization, which tracks infectious diseases and sends out health workers to vaccinate people in developing countries, affect people all over the world.

(C) At the regional scale there are many supranational organizations which fulfill political, economic, and social roles. The European Union is a political and economic organization which regulates borders, immigration, passports, and political arguments between member countries while also regulating trade, both between member countries and with the outside world. NATO is a purely political alliance that began after World War II to protect member countries from communism but has since changed into a peacekeeping force in Europe. Other economic examples include international trade agreements, such as NAFTA between the United States, Mexico and Canada, and OPEC, the Organization of Oil Producing Countries, which sets oil production amounts and prices for its members, thereby controlling the price of oil.

Rubric: This answer is worth nine points. In Part A, the student receives two points, one for the definition provided and one for the explanation. In Part B, the student receives three points, one for the definition and one for each example. In Part C, the student receives two points for each of the examples/explanations provided.
Chapter: 12: The Political Ordering of Space
Section: 12.2
AP Topic: 4.9 Challenges to Sovereignty

Human Impacts on the Environment

AP Introduction

Chapter 13 introduces students to environmental geography. Chapter 13 does not have a directly corresponding unit in the Advanced Placement Human Geography course framework. This chapter draws from parts of the seven units that contain environmentally oriented material. These are listed by course framework topic number and name:

- 1.5 Human Environmental Interaction

  Enduring Understanding: Geographers analyze relationships among and between places to reveal important spatial patterns.

- 2.2 Consequences of Population Distribution

  Enduring Understanding: Understanding where and how people live is essential to understanding global cultural, political, and economic patterns.

- 5.10 Consequences of Agricultural Practices

  Enduring Understanding: Agricultural production and consumption patterns vary in different locations, presenting different environmental, social, economic, and cultural opportunities and challenges.

- 5.11 Challenges of Contemporary Agriculture

  Enduring Understanding: Agricultural production and consumption patterns vary in different locations, presenting different environmental, social, economic, and cultural opportunities and challenges.

- 6.8 Urban Sustainability

  Enduring Understanding: The attitudes and values of a population, as well as the balance of power within that population, are reflected in the built landscape.

- 6.11 Challenges of Urban Sustainability

  Enduring Understanding: Urban areas face unique economic, political, cultural, and environmental challenges.

- 7.8 Sustainable Development

  Enduring Understanding: Environmental problems stemming from industrialization may be remedied through sustainable development strategies.

AP Concepts and Themes

Chapter Overview

This chapter contains fundamentals of the study of environmental geography, including the following:

- How humans and the environment influence each other
- The impact of population distribution and density upon society
- The way in which agriculture is practiced alters the environment, sometimes with significant negative consequences for society
- Present day agricultural practices invite critical analysis of their sustainability
- Urban design for sustainability
- Challenges to sustainable urban living and policy responses
- Economic development needs to be sustainable to avoid environmental degradation and loss of short-term gains

Learning Objectives

- Explain how major geographic concepts illustrate spatial relationships.
- Explain how population distribution and density affect society and the environment.
- Explain how agricultural practices have environmental and societal consequences.
- Explain challenges and debates related to the changing nature of contemporary agriculture and food production practices.
- Identify the different urban design initiatives and practices.
- Explain the effects of different urban design initiatives and practices.
- Describe the effectiveness of different attempts to address urban sustainability challenges.
- Explain how sustainability principles relate to and impact industrialization and spatial development.

Key Words

Use the terms below with a ▮ to focus your study of AP Human Geography key words in this chapter.

acid precipitation	▮ environmental determinism	Not in My Backyard (NIMBY)
▮ aquaculture	environmental justice	ozone
aquifer	environmental pollution	▮ pastoral nomadism
atmosphere	fallowing	▮ possibilism
biome	▮ genetically modified organism (GMO)	rotation
biosphere	▮ greenbelts	▮ shifting cultivation
▮ brownfield	▮ global climate change	soil
▮ carrying capacity	greenhouse effect	soil erosion
dead zones	hazardous waste	▮ soil salinization
▮ deforestation	hydrologic cycle	▮ sprawl
▮ desertification	hydrosphere	▮ sustainability
ecosphere	IPAT equation	sustainable development
ecosystem	lithosphere	terracing
▮ ecotourism	▮ natural resource	transboundary river basins
environment	▮ New Urbanism	▮ urban growth boundary

Note to the Teacher

The Key Word *urban growth boundary* is included in the AP Course Framework, but this concept is not discussed in depth in the Bjelland Student Edition. In the context of human geography, an *urban growth boundary refers* to geographical boundaries placed around a city to limit suburban growth within that city.

AP Chapter Discussion and Activities

Understanding Challenges to Urban Sustainability

AP ESSENTIAL KNOWLEDGE: Challenges to urban sustainability include suburban sprawl, sanitation, climate change, air and water quality, the large ecological footprint of cities, and energy use.

TEACH: *Tell students that acid precipitation is a significant problem in some parts of the United States and Canada. To students it may seem like an obscure, distant problem. Use Figure 13.9 on page 438 and Figure 13.11 on page 439 help review the causes and effects of acid precipitation in the United States.*

Ask students to look for signs of acid precipitation in their communities. This may be visible in the erosion of stone surfaces, such as gravestones, statues, and the steps of older, prominent buildings, like libraries, museums, and government administration centers. Explain that the impact of acid precipitation on vegetation or surface water bodies may be harder to discern, so a search of the Internet for newspaper articles might be necessary to identify these impacts. Students should summarize their findings in a brief oral presentation. Presentations should include images that show examples of the effects of acid precipitation.

Identifying the Effects of Global Climate Change

AP ESSENTIAL KNOWLEDGE: Sustainable development policies attempt to remedy problems stemming from natural-resource depletion, mass consumption, the effects of pollution, and the impact of climate change.

TEACH: *Remind students that global climate change (GCC) is expected to affect different parts of the planet in diverse ways. Ask students to investigate how GCC is predicted to affect their region, state or metropolitan area. Various scientific organizations, weather forecasters, or disaster relief authorities may have been quoted in the mass media on the regional or local impacts of GCC.*

Have students create a large poster to display their findings, which might include illustrations such as photos, maps, schematic diagrams, and data tables. Extend this activity with a class discussion on the causes and consequences of climate change in other parts of the world.

Analyzing the Environmental Effects of Development

AP ESSENTIAL KNOWLEDGE: Sustainable development policies attempt to remedy problems stemming from natural-resource depletion, mass consumption, the effects of pollution, and the impact of climate change.

TEACH: *Discuss with students how economic development brings advantages to some individuals and societies but with the unfortunate by-product of pollution and waste. Individuals and neighborhoods seek the benefits of development but wish to avoid the costs by living away from noxious facilities like landfills, recycling centers, and power plants. This resistance to having unpleasant, if not harmful, sites in close proximity to one's home is called Not In My Backyard (NIMBY).*

Ask students to make a simple sketch map of their community showing the location of environmentally concerning sites. The map should label some major roads, mass transportation lines, and buildings as landmarks. Using their completed sketch maps, students should then look at the spatial distribution of these sites. Provide the following questions to help guide students' analysis: Are they found in all areas of the community? If not, where are they found? How can the distribution be explained? Is the pattern purely the result of discriminatory siting practices or might other factors play a role?

Have students create a short presentation to share their maps, any photos taken of environmentally important sites, and their own analysis of the pattern of these facilities.

Determining the Effects of Agriculture on the Environment

AP ESSENTIAL KNOWLEDGE: Environmental effects of agriculture land use include pollution, land cover change, desertification, soil salinization, and conservation efforts.
Agricultural practices—including slash and burn, terraces, irrigation, deforestation, draining wetlands, shifting cultivation, and pastoral nomadism—alter the landscape.

TEACH: *Remind students that agriculture is vital to supplying the planet's roughly seven billion people with daily nutrition. While all forms of agriculture have an impact on the environment, modern commercial agriculture is especially impactful.*

Ask students to form small groups and consider the various techniques that commercial agriculture uses to produce enormous quantities of plants and animals for human consumption. Each student in the group could be assigned one or more techniques to research, e.g. use of chemical fertilizers, use of heavy machinery, use of only a handful of varieties of a staple crop, like corn. Students should share their findings within the group and then synthesize that information into a statement about the overall impact of that type of agriculture on the environment. Other groups of students could be assigned to consider the impact of subsistence farming as practiced in developing countries or specialized types of agriculture, such as aquaculture or indoor urban farms. Groups representing different types of agriculture should share their results with the class in the form of an oral presentation or poster.

Researching the Impact of Population Growth on the Environment

AP ESSENTIAL KNOWLEDGE: Population distribution and density affect the environment and natural resources; this is known as carrying capacity.

TEACH: *Tell students that about two-thirds of the planet is covered by water, and some of the remaining land areas have climates that are not favorable to human settlement. Thus, much of the Earth's human population is clustered in a handful of densely populated regions. At the local scale, major urban areas around the world have populations more than one, five, or even ten million people. As populations and density grow, how is the environment affected?*

Have students work in small groups to research a place—a country like Bangladesh or the Netherlands or an urban area like New York City, Mexico City, or Shanghai. For their chosen area of study, groups should consider the following questions: (1) How many people live there? (2) What is the approximate population density? (3) What environmental impacts are present in the study area, and how are they a function of population density? (4) What steps are being taken to remedy the environmental impacts? (5) If no action is being taken to protect the environment, why not?

Remind students that basic information about population size and density is often available from organizations like the UN or the CIA. Global or national environmental organizations might have done some studies of the selected areas, upon which students can draw. Major media outlets like the New York Times *or the BBC might also contain stories with relevant material. Each group should use their findings to create a presentation for the class. After presentations have been made, make time for a class discussion to talk about similarities and differences among the areas of study.*

Evaluating Urban Design

AP ESSENTIAL KNOWLEDGE: Praise for urban design initiatives includes the reduction of sprawl, improved walkability and transportation, improved and diverse housing options, improved livability and promotion of sustainable options. Criticisms include increased housing costs, possible de facto segregation, and the potential loss of historical or place character.

TEACH: *Explain to students that while sustainability in urban places can be partly addressed by designing individual buildings to be more energy efficient, the design of entire neighborhoods should also be taken into consideration.*

Ask students to evaluate a neighborhood within their community or a nearby urban place. Encourage them to use the following questions to guide their evaluation: What characteristics are visible indicating that sustainability is a concern to the city or town? For example, are there dedicated bike travel lanes on the roads? Is there mass transit available? Are there special parking spaces and charging stations for electric vehicles? Is the neighborhood pedestrian-friendly with businesses located within walking distance of residences? How much green space, in the form of parks, playing fields, or other open areas, exists for recreation and to prevent flooding? Students should document their observations by creating an annotated sketch map that includes photos.

AP Chapter Feature Answer Key

Geography and Citizenship

1. Students' papers should clearly defend their position on the issues and provide logical evidence to support. Papers should include correct grammar, style, and punctuation.

2. Remind students that local news media coverage may be helpful in identifying environmental hazards in the local community. Presentations should include maps and other visuals, as well as evidence of research using reputable sources.

AP Test Practice Answer Key

Below are the Bjelland end-of-chapter AP Test Practice questions along with their answers, feedback, and rubrics.

Multiple Choice Questions

1. People practicing sustainable development should

(A) use only the water available to them through groundwater that is replenished from rainfall and snowmelt.

(B) harvest large amounts of fish to avoid overgrazing of their land caused by raising livestock.

(C) practice slash and burn agriculture to gain as many resources from the land as possible in a short amount of time.

(D) use aquafarming techniques to raise only the species of fish that are the most profitable.

(E) use fossil fuels and plastics instead of renewable resources.

Answer: A

Feedback: Practicing sustainable development means doing things that will keep the earth in its present shape or make it even more livable in the future. Using less water, so that the amount available is replenished naturally rather than piping it in from elsewhere, harvesting only the number of fish that will allow the fish to replenish their populations, and harvesting various types of fish instead of only one kind are all sustainable practices. Slash and burn agriculture as it is practiced today destroys rainforests, while use of fossil fuels pollutes the environment and uses up scarce world resources, both of which are unsustainable practices.

Chapter: 13: Human Impacts on the Environment

Section: 13.1

AP Topic: 7.8 Sustainable Development

2. According to the maps in Figure 13.2 on page 434, because of the rotation of the Earth and the tilt of its axis,

(A) it is always warmer in the sea than on the land.

(B) the temperature in January is warmer in the southern hemisphere, while the temperature in July is warmer in the northern hemisphere.

(C) the temperature fluctuates randomly between hot and cold in both hemispheres.

(D) the temperature in January in the northern hemisphere does not get as cold as it does in July in the southern hemisphere.

(E) people living in Australia experience winter in January and summer in July like everyone else in the world.

Answer: B

Feedback: Since the Earth is tilted as it rotates around the sun, the northern hemisphere gets more direct sun's rays in July and is therefore hotter. The opposite is true of the southern hemisphere, which experiences summer in January and winter in July.

Chapter: 13: Human Impacts on the Environment

Section: 13.1

AP Topic: 1.5 Human Environment Interaction

3. The problem of air pollution is evident in all of the following situations EXCEPT

(A) indoor pollutants from using cook fires inside the house cause lung ailments and death in developing countries.

(B) industrial pollution of air and rivers as developing countries industrialize cause death and illness of people and livestock.

(C) cities experience days of bad air quality due to the burning of fossil fuels in power plants and cars.

(D) the dumping of tons of trash in landfills and in the oceans causes fish and marine mammals to become ill and die.

(E) forests are devastated and waterways are contaminated worldwide due to pollutants in the atmosphere that are brought to earth by acid rain.

Answer: D

Feedback: All the above pollute the air except for D, which pollutes the land and water.

Chapter: 13: Human Impacts on the Environment

Section: 13.1

AP Topic: 6.11 Challenges of Urban Sustainability

4. According to Table 13.1 on page 442, the countries that have the most impact on climate change are

   (A) rapidly industrializing countries with large populations, like China and India.

   (B) countries with a high standard of living like the United States, which has not curbed its usage of fossil fuels.

   (C) countries with cold climates, like Russia and Canada, that can burn fossil fuels for heat.

   (D) developing countries with small populations, like Ghana and Costa Rica.

   (E) European countries, like the United Kingdom and Germany.

Answer: A

Feedback: Countries with a high standard of living tend to burn more fossil fuels per capita, and, therefore, emit more carbon into the atmosphere. It is possible, however, to lower this impact, as seen by the statistics on Germany, the UK and Japan. Climate has less of an impact than does level of industrialization and population. Countries that are industrializing rapidly and increasing the standard of living of their large populations, like China and India, have the most impact on carbon emissions which cause climate change.

Chapter: 13: Human Impacts on the Environment

Section: 13.1

AP Topic: 7.8 Sustainable Development

5. Major concerns raised by tropical deforestation include all of the following EXCEPT

   (A) forests help maintain the oxygen and carbon balance of the planet.

   (B) loss of habitat will affect biodiversity of species by causing mass extinctions.

   (C) land used for farming provides food for millions of people.

   (D) erosion of soil is rapid once trees are cut down, and the land quickly becomes infertile.

   (E) the rise in temperature due to lack of ground cover leads to heat waves and other climate related events.

Answer: C

Feedback: All the above answers are negative consequences of deforestation except C which is a positive consequence, at least for a short while. After a year or two of farming, the thin soil of a former rainforest becomes depleted and unusable. Without ground cover, it dries up and blows away.

Chapter: 13: Human Impacts on the Environment

Section: 13.2

AP Topic: 5.10 Consequences of Agricultural Practices

6. The expansion or intensification of areas of degraded or destroyed soil and vegetation in arid and semi-arid regions of the world is called

   (A) global climate change.

   (B) desertification.

   (C) erosion.

   (D) slash and burn agriculture.

   (E) transhumance.

Answer: B

Feedback: Desertification is the process by which land becomes a desert. In many parts of the world, deserts are growing due to overgrazing by livestock, slash and burn agriculture, and global climate change.

Chapter: 13: Human Impacts on the Environment

Section: 13.2

AP Topic: 5.10 Consequences of Agricultural Practices

7. The building of dams in developing countries is made more problematic by

   (A) retaliation by people whose homes were flooded.

   (B) environmental groups protesting the loss of animal habitats.

   (C) quick growth of tropical plants, such as water hyacinth, that clogs reservoirs.

   (D) deforestation of river banks and excessive rains that cause dams to burst.

   (E) lack of infrastructure to transport electricity produced to the people who need it.

Answer: C

Feedback: Problems associated with dam building include the flooding of people's homes and the destruction of animal habitats and biological diversity. Protests by homeowners and environmental groups have had little to no effect on dam building. Lack of infrastructure to carry the electricity has not been a problem. Deforestation causes erosion of riverbanks, which leads to reservoirs filling up with silt, not excessive rainfall and burst dams. Answer C, however, the quick growth of tropical plants, is speeded up even more due to excessive plant materials in the reservoirs from flooded trees.

Chapter: 13: Human Impacts on the Environment

Section: 13.2

AP Topic: 1.5 Human Environmental Interaction

8. The use of irrigation

(A) causes areas downstream to experience drought conditions.

(B) has allowed the production of 90 percent of the world's crops on just 17 percent of the land.

(C) means that in many places groundwater is being pumped out sustainably at a lower rate than it is being replenished.

(D) is unnecessary except in the driest areas of the world.

(E) is an inexpensive way for farmers to expand the arable portion of their land.

Answer: A

Feedback: The use of irrigation and other aspects of Green Revolution technology allows farmers to produce about 40 percent of the world's crops on 17 percent of the land. It means, however, that in many places groundwater is being pumped out unsustainably, not being replenished by rain or snowmelt. Irrigation is time consuming and expensive, and it uses water from rivers and streams that might be needed downstream. This can cause drought conditions and even the drying up of bodies of water like the Aral Sea.

Chapter: 13: Human Impacts on the Environment

Section: 13.3

AP Topic: 5.10 Consequences of Agricultural Practices

9. Coastal dead zones are caused by

(A) rivers drying up due to overuse of groundwater by irrigation projects upstream.

(B) die offs of birds, fish, and marine mammals.

(C) red tides made up of toxic algae.

(D) runoff of chemicals used by farmers and animal waste from feedlots.

(E) industrial waste dumped into waterways.

Answer: D

Feedback: Coastal dead zones are usually found at the mouth of rivers and are caused by agricultural runoff. Fertilizer and animal waste from commercial farming contain nutrients that help plants grow, but too much causes overgrowth of algae and other plants that use up all the oxygen in the water, causing dead zones. One of the largest is at the mouth of the Mississippi River in the Gulf of Mexico. Industrial waste pollutes waterways, too, but does not cause the same overgrowth of plant life.

Chapter: 13: Human Impacts on the Environment

Section: 13.3

AP Topic: 5.10 Consequences of Agricultural Practices

10. Radioactive and other hazardous wastes

(A) are disposed of in lagoons or pits to keep them from contaminating groundwater.

(B) are not dangerous to humans or the environment as long as they are disposed of in the ocean where the large amount of water disperses the waste.

(C) come from military and nuclear facilities, not from civilian sources.

(D) are rarely exported to developing countries, which do not have the facilities to deal with them.

(E) are incinerated or disposed of today in facilities in the desert or in lined landfills to keep contamination out of groundwater sources.

Answer: E

Feedback: In the past, toxic wastes were disposed of in lagoons and pits, but groundwater contamination became a problem. Now they are incinerated or disposed of in lined landfills, which do not allow the contents to leak into water supplies. Radioactive waste comes from civilian and military sources as well as from nuclear power plants. It must be disposed of very carefully in extremely dry areas far away from human habitation because it is radioactive for such a long time.

Chapter: 13: Human Impacts on the Environment

Section: 13.4

AP Topic: 1.5 Human Environmental Interaction

Free Response Questions

1. Study the diagram in Figure 13.13 on page 441 and the graphs in Figure 13.16 on page 444 to help you answer Parts A and B below.

   (A) Identify and explain three geographic effects of global climate change.

   (B) Explain one cause of climate change and one solution to the problem.

   (A) One effect of global climate change is the melting of ice in the Arctic and Antarctic, which will cause rising sea levels. This in turn will flood low-lying coastal areas, like the densely populated delta of the Ganges River in Bangladesh. Some islands, such as Vanuatu, may be totally under water. A second effect of global climate change is drought conditions in areas that are already very dry, such as the desert southwest of the United States, sub-Saharan Africa, the Middle East, Mexico, and Southern Europe. This will in turn affect agriculture and cause more wildfires. A third effect of global climate change is that the number and intensity of tropical storms will increase, hitting already poverty-stricken parts of the world such as the Caribbean and Indonesia.

   (B) Climate change is caused by excessive amounts of carbon dioxide and other gases being released into the atmosphere. These gases keep heat from escaping the earth's atmosphere, so it builds up, affecting weather patterns around the world. One solution to the problem is to drastically cut the amount of carbon we are emitting by cutting our usage of fossil fuels. Switching to wind energy like many European countries and buying more electric cars are a start. Many countries have joined the Kyoto Protocol and the Paris Accord, agreeing to cut energy usage and carbon emissions. The United States, however, which ranks third in the world for energy use per capita, never ratified the Kyoto Treaty and recently pulled out of the Paris Accord.

   Rubric: This is worth seven points, three for Part A, and two each for the cause of climate change and a solution to it.
   Chapter: 13: Human Impacts on the Environment
   Section: 13.2
   AP Topic: 1.5 Human Environmental Interaction

2. Explain three methods farmers can use to combat soil erosion.

   Farmers can combat the problem of soil erosion in several ways. First, rotating crops can preserve soil fertility and stave off erosion by keeping a ground cover planted always. Different kinds of crops use different nutrients in the soil, and some even replenish the soil's nutrients. Since the soil does not become infertile, it can continue to be used. Since there are plants in the ground all the time, their roots hold the soil, keep water in, and prevent erosion. Second, farmers can leave a field to lie fallow for a year or two, allowing it to replenish its moisture in semi-arid lands or to replenish soil fertility in rainforest areas. A third method of preventing soil erosion is by terracing hilly or mountainous terrain so water does not run straight down the hill, but instead pools on terraces, nourishing the plants.

   Rubric: This answer is worth six points, two for each method of stopping erosion.
   Chapter: 13: Human Impacts on the Environment
   Section: 13.2
   AP Topic: 5.10 Consequences of Agricultural Practices

3. Define the concepts of *environmental racism* and *environmental justice* and explain them using examples from the United States and two other countries.

   Environmental racism is when the majority population uses land where minorities live to dump wastes, run a pipeline through, or in some other way discriminates against the minority environmentally. If it is something wealthy people do not want in their back yard (NIMBY), they force minorities to have it in theirs. Environmental justice is the idea that environmental practices should be done fairly, in a way that impacts all groups of people equally. An example of environmental racism from the United States occurred in Warren County, North Carolina, when the mostly African American residents discovered that their neighborhood had been proposed as the site of a hazardous waste dump. Protests led to hundreds of arrests. Taking the case to court failed and the dump was built, exposing many residents to a dangerous situation. The same types of environmental injustice happen all over the world. Many times, it is the poor who are discriminated against, not another ethnic group. In Johannesburg, South Africa, an area of "informal housing" (i.e., an urban slum) grew up near a gold mine. The area where the refuse from the mine was dumped expanded further and further until it was only 30 yards from poor people's homes. Dust from the drying mine tailings is extremely toxic and causes irreversible lung damage. The United States and other countries are trying to do something to bring about more environmental justice. In 1992 the Office of Environmental Justice was founded as part of the EPA. In Louisiana, primarily poor black residents of an area along the Mississippi River known as "Cancer Alley" successfully got a chemical plant moved 48 miles upriver. It is difficult to get more industrialized states to stop dumping their wastes on developing countries' land. The Organization of African Unity adopted a resolution in 1988 condemning the dumping of foreign wastes on that continent, and the Basel Convention on hazardous waste shipping and disposal went into effect in 1992, although the USA never ratified it. The EU only allows hazardous wastes to be shipped to other EU countries that have facilities to safely process it, but the United States ships most of its e-waste to China, India, Pakistan, and other developing countries for recycling. Unregulated recycling in developing countries leads to toxic exposure and environmental damage.

   Rubric: This answer is worth eight points, one point each for the definitions of *environmental racism* and *environmental justice*, and two points each for the explanations and examples. Note that in the answer, the United States is used for two examples, South Africa is used for one, and the OAU and Basel, Switzerland, are used for another. China, India, and Pakistan are also mentioned.
   Chapter: 13: Human Impacts on the Environment
   Section: 13.4
   AP Topic: 1.5 Human Environmental Interaction